John Marshall
*Defender of
the Constitution*

Francis N. Stites

John Marshall

Defender of the Constitution

Edited by Oscar Handlin

Little, Brown and Company · *Boston* · *Toronto*

To Joan, Madelaine, and Audrey

HAL

*Published simultaneously in Canada
by Little, Brown & Company (Canada) Limited*

PRINTED IN THE UNITED STATES OF AMERICA

Editor's Preface

The Constitution of the United States, composed in 1787 and ratified soon after, survived almost intact into the last decades of the twentieth century. The first ten amendments were explanatory supplements rather than changes, and did not really alter the intention of the framers. Down to the Civil War Americans added only two other amendments; and those adopted since 1870 did not really alter the structure of the government, although they affected the rights of individuals under it. This record of durability is without parallel in modern states.

The Constitution remained stable despite abundant conflict within the country, both social and sectional. It survived also despite the profound mutations that transformed an agricultural and mercantile nation of a few million people along the Atlantic seaboard into a continental power resting on an industrial base. The Constitution did not remain inert; it responded to new conditions. Indeed its longevity derived from its capacity to absorb change and to adjust to conflict.

The members of the constitutional convention of 1787 had not expected their handiwork to survive as it did, for they assumed that each generation would decide upon its own frame of government. The surprising longevity of the Constitution owed a great deal to the role that John Marshall helped to fashion for the Supreme Court. That body under his leadership became the central custodian of constitutional doctrine, permitting some changes, restraining, all the while developing a sense of the limits of what was permissible, what not.

Marshall's influence did not spring from his technical learning in the law, but rather from his experience in eighteenth-century Virginia politics. Associated with the landed gentry who ruled that province and state, like Washington, Jefferson, and Madison, he early learned the value of government by law. In addition, the War of Independence early developed his love of country and his understanding of the qualities that held its political system together.

There was something more, however. This careful account of Marshall's life by Professor Stites offers useful insights into the qualities of mind that enabled the justice to locate particular cases in the context of broad generalizations, and thus to explore the relationship of power to law.

OSCAR HANDLIN

Contents

Acknowledgments

THROUGHOUT THIS WORK I have leaned heavily on the backs of others. Simple acknowledgment of my debt to the scores of Marshall scholars from whose work I have gleaned most of my raw material and insight seems woefully inadequate. I owe a special debt to Maurice G. Baxter, my teacher and model of the careful scholar. Joyce A. Appleby and Robert Filner read portions of my manuscript and provided the happy blend of encouragement and merciless criticism one hopes for from colleagues. The heaviest burden fell to my wife, Joan, who graciously accepted John Marshall into her life and sustained me at every step. Finally, my daughters Madelaine and Audrey exhibited a persistence in asking when I would finish that entitles them to see their names in print.

FRANCIS N. STITES

John Marshall

Defender of the Constitution

I

The Virginian

1755–1783

JOHN MARSHALL was a Virginian—by birth, upbringing, disposition, and property. His thirty-four years as chief justice of the United States overshadowed his early life, yet the chief justice always remained what his early years had made of him. The world of his youth left enduring marks upon his character.

*   *   *

Eighteenth-century Virginia was a thinly settled, stable but expansive agricultural society with well-defined classes and a firm attachment to government by the rich, the well-born, and the able. At its head was the gentry, a loose collection of aristocrats of the Tidewater region and aspiring, ambitious lesser planters who struggled for entry to the upper stratum of the society. The pathway to success had long been established. Connection with the gentry through birth or marriage was a necessary first step, but wealth was also necessary, and the quickest and surest way to it was through the acquisition of land. As the basis of the right to vote and of officeholding, land was the springboard to political influence. But political influence had to be earned by capable performance in a series of moves from posts in the county courts through positions in the militia and the House of Burgesses to the higher provincial positions. Thomas Marshall, John Marshall's father, exemplified the ambitious and successful lesser planter. In less than a decade he parlayed a marriage, good connections, and land speculation into a role as one of the leading men of his county.

Virginia's Northern Neck region was fertile and free of the swamps and fevers of the Tidewater farther south. The area had long seemed a good place to settle, build a home, rear a family, and make a fortune. So it appeared to Thomas Marshall in 1752 when he moved with his new wife and two slaves to Germantown in Prince William County. His wife, Mary Randolph Keith, was the daughter of a minister of the Church of England and the great-granddaughter of William Randolph and Mary Isham, a couple whose numerous descendants earned them the fanciful name of the "Adam and Eve of Virginia." Through Mary, Thomas had links to the Jeffersons, the Randolphs, and the Lees, who were among Virginia's first families. At Germantown he became assistant to George Washington, his longtime friend, who had just been appointed surveyor for the Fairfax estate, which embraced most of the Northern Neck. That friendship, that job, that Fairfax name and estate were of continuing importance to Thomas Marshall and to his son John, the eldest of fifteen children, born September 24, 1755, in his father's cottage.

When John was ten, the family moved about thirty miles farther west to a densely forested, picturesque valley in the Blue Ridge Mountains called The Hollow. Using family connections to lease 350 acres from the Lee family, Thomas Marshall built a substantial if not pretentious one-and-a-half-story frame house. By January 1773 his growing prosperity enabled him to purchase 1700 acres in a more favorable location, where he built Oak Hill, a two-story frame house—not a Mount Vernon, a Monticello, or a Gunston Hall but nonetheless impressive for that area. He remained at Oak Hill until 1783 when he moved to Kentucky and built an even larger fortune. At the time he left Virginia his estate of several thousand acres and twenty slaves was one of the largest in the county.

Membership in the gentry required participation in the government. Thomas Marshall's service began in 1759 when Fauquier County split off from Prince William County. In that year the "President and Masters of the College of William and Mary" appointed him county surveyor, an important position for a land speculator. It imposed the obligation to divide the county into districts and to list the residents for tax purposes.

In the same year he became a justice of the peace, the most important appointive position in the local government of eighteenth-century Virginia. The appointment marked the establishment of the Marshall family among the gentry. Justices of the peace were always gentlemen and men of wealth. They had immense local power. Individually they settled minor disputes and issued court orders. Collectively they constituted the county court, a practical school in the uses of power. Service on the court kept the justices in touch with county life and enabled them to observe the effects of general policies set by the House of Burgesses at Williamsburg.

The court was the governing body of the county, exercising executive, legislative, and judicial power. On their monthly court days the justices gathered at the county seat and passed upon all civil and criminal matters—the building of roads and public works, taxes, elections, public health, and questions involving orphans, bastards, and slaves. People flocked to the county seat, some to transact business at court, others to transact business amidst the assembled crowds. In this county fair atmosphere Virginians met and governed themselves in a curious blend of aristocracy and democracy. Experience at the court trained the successful young gentleman.

John Marshall was later one of few to rise to prominence without service on the county courts, but they left a powerful impression on him. When he was seventy-four he wrote that "less disquiet and less of ill-feeling between man and man" existed in Virginia than in any part of America. He ascribed that state of affairs "to the practical operation of our County Courts. The magistrates . . . act in the spirit of peacemakers, and allay, rather than excite the small disputes and differences which will sometimes arise among neighbours. It is certainly much owing to this, that so much harmony prevails amongst us."

The court chose every county official either by direct appointment or through recommendations to the governor. The court also had great power over elections. The sheriff, commissioned on its recommendation, managed the elections; the justices rotated as sheriff for two-year terms. Thomas Marshall served as sheriff from 1767 to 1769. Toward the end of his term he demonstrated graphically the power he commanded. While still sheriff he announced his candidacy for the House of Burgesses and timed the elections to assure his victory—an action finely attuned to the specific demands of Virginia political life.

Membership in the House of Burgesses was the next step for an ambitious gentleman. The capital at Williamsburg offered the opportunity for exercising a voice in provincial affairs, but service there did not lessen a man's ties to the county. Reelection demanded approval by the freeholders and justices. With only two brief interludes, Thomas Marshall served as burgess from 1761 to 1775, eloquent testimony to his continued rise to power and influence. He had frequent personal and official contact with other aspiring or established gentlemen—Patrick Henry, George Washington, George Wythe, and Thomas Jefferson.

Elected vestryman of the newly organized parish of Leeds in 1769 and organizer of the Fauquier County militia in 1775, he had clearly laid the solid foundation for his son's later success. John Marshall later spoke of his father as a man who possessed "scarcely any fortune, and [who] had received a very limited education;—but he was a man to whom nature had been bountiful, and who had assiduously improved her gifts."

Young John Marshall received a very limited education—one year's study of the classics at fourteen and a few months study under a private clergyman. In Virginia, except for those few exceptions such as Thomas Jefferson and James Madison, education was not formal but was largely a private, familial affair. Men were educated, as Thomas Marshall had been, through participation.

In a Virginia where land and politics determined a man's fortune, John Marshall's education was well-suited to meet those demands. From his father he acquired "an early taste for history and poetry," the rudimentary skills of reading and writing, and no doubt some practice in surveying. At age twelve he had transcribed Alexander Pope's *Essay on Man* and some of Pope's moral essays, and he may have read Milton, Dryden, and Shakespeare. One year at the Reverend Archibald Campbell's academy about one hundred miles from Oak Hill and the time spent under the instruction of his tutor, the Reverend James Thomson, gave him enough familiarity with the classics that by age fifteen he was reading Horace and Livy in the Latin. In 1772 Thomas Marshall added to his library—whose volumes were probably no more in number than the children in his house—a four-volume set of the American edition of Sir William Blackstone's *Commentaries on the Laws of England,* from which young John began to read. More important to his education were the attitudes, information, and values John gleaned from observing his father, from accompanying him on court days, and from general participation in the life of Fauquier County. Through this exposure he acquired the manners and habits of a Virginia gentleman—a sense of duty, a fondness for games and athletic contests, a gracious hospitality, and a disarming, engaging personality. These qualities, in addition to a sloppiness in appearance that betrayed his yeoman origin, distinguished him throughout his life.

War dramatically altered young Marshall's life. In the spring of 1774 Parliament, outraged by the Boston Tea Party, retaliated with a series of punitive measures against Massachusetts. These restraints, known as the Coercive Acts, roused and united the colonies as nothing had done since the Stamp Act crisis of 1765. In September the First Continental Congress met to concert opposition to Mother England's depredations. In March 1775 the fiery Patrick Henry proclaimed peace at an end and delivered his "Give me liberty or give me death" peroration. The following month brought clashes at Lexington and Concord, and the colonies everywhere raised militia units.

Through it all Americans claimed only protection of their rights as loyal British subjects. Seeking not independence but the continuation of the self-rule they had enjoyed, they finally came to see, as Marshall later said, that "to profess allegiance for a monarch with whom they were at open war, was an absurdity too great to be long continued."

Barely nineteen when the Continental Congress assembled, John Marshall engaged in the swiftly moving train of events with all the zeal and enthusiasm of his age. He had grown up with the controversy. Agricultural Virginia had not manifested the frenetic mob violence of urban Massachusetts. In the 1760s her deceptively placid outward appearance masked a declining economy. Falling prices, currency shortages, and persistent planter indebtedness meant that even great landholders had difficulty meeting their obligations. England added to the growing anxiety with actions such as the Proclamation of 1763, which closed lands west of the mountains to settlement and threatened the ambitions and claims of a great many land-hungry Virginians.

The Stamp Act had upset Virginians and fired the colonies into united opposition. As a member of the House of Burgesses, Thomas Marshall had been among those voting against that measure in the famous meeting at the Raleigh Tavern in Williamsburg. When the hated law was repealed, cool heads again prevailed, and gentlemen settled back to tend their estates, considering themselves loyal citizens of the most powerful nation on earth. Still there were lingering difficulties. Even modest and reluctant patriots such as George Washington began to talk after the 1767 Townshend Duties about the ultimate need to resort to arms to protect property and privilege. Thomas Marshall, like his friend, was not eager for a break, but he resisted British efforts to assert sovereignty over the colonies. He was a member of the Virginia Convention of 1775 and supported Patrick Henry's call for arming the colony in self-defense. Back at Fauquier he had spoken excitedly of the convention and of Henry's eloquence. It was a time, John Marshall recalled, "when a love of union and resistance to the claims of Great Britain were the inseparable inmates of the same bosom;—when patriotism and a strong fellow feeling with our suffering fellow citizens of Boston were identical."

Excited by this atmosphere John Marshall spent more time studying the manual of arms and the political tracts of the day than the classics or Blackstone. In 1775 the royal governor, Lord Dunmore, agitated Virginians more than did Parliament. In April he had seized the gunpowder in the Williamsburg public arsenal and had spoken of freeing slaves to fight rebellion. Such talk cut to the quick, and some militia units threatened a march on the capital.

The Fauquier County militia, with John Marshall as lieutenant, gathered in a field about ten miles from Oak Hill in early May. Assuming command in the absence of the captain, Marshall made a lasting impression on the assembled minutemen. His uniform of a pale blue hunting shirt and leggings, "fringed with white," accentuated his lean, six-foot frame. Beneath a round black hat with a bucktail cockade beamed a round face, "nearly a circle," a heavy head of thick "raven-black" hair, and, most striking, black eyes, "strong and penetrating, beaming with intelligence and good nature." After drilling the company for one hour and addressing them for another, Marshall spent the remainder of the day pitching quoits (round stone discs) and running races with his men.

Piercing black eyes, a fondness and an aptitude for quoits and races, simplicity, "gaiety of heart and manliness of spirit"—these traits defined the essential John Marshall.

As he walked the ten miles back to Oak Hill that May evening the fever was abating in Virginia. Governor Dunmore had paid for the powder and removed both it and his person from the capital to ships anchored off Norfolk. The historic Second Continental Congress had met and, amid arguments over the wisdom of independence, had appointed George Washington commander in chief of the Continental army and had sent him to aid the distressed patriots in Boston. The Congress adopted John Dickinson's "Olive Branch Petition" just as news of Bunker Hill reached Philadelphia. This deferential document expressed the urgent desire of loyal Americans for a restoration of former harmony with England and simultaneously set forth the necessary resort to arms if reconciliation were impossible. King George III rejected the petition and in August proclaimed a state of rebellion in all his American colonies.

As the threat of armed conflict mounted, Virginia appointed Patrick Henry commander in chief and issued a call to arms. Among more than a thousand volunteers who filled the ranks by late September was the Culpeper Minutemen Battalion, a 350-man outfit formed by the three contiguous counties of Orange, Culpeper, and Fauquier. Thomas Marshall held the rank of major; his son John was a lieutenant. They had assembled on September 1 outside the town of Fairfax and, wearing the same blue hunting shirts, carrying tomahawks and long rifles, had marched off to Williamsburg under a flag emblazoned with a segmented rattlesnake and the motto "Don't Tread on Me." From Williamsburg they were ordered to the lower country to defend it against a small force commanded by Dunmore.

Dunmore in October had begun to raid the Virginia coast with his fleet based at Norfolk. In November 1775 he had declared martial law, proclaimed all who would not rally to him traitors, and again repeated his decision to free slaves who would fight for the king. At a place called Great Bridge, about twelve miles north of Norfolk, John Marshall saw his first combat on December 9, 1775. Without a single loss the Virginians inflicted a decisive defeat on a force of over five hundred British grenadiers, some loyalists, and Negroes who had heeded Dunmore's call. Dunmore retired to Norfolk. Marshall and the minutemen followed and were there when the retreating British set the town on fire. The British occupation of Virginia had come to an end. The colony was secure, and the minutemen returned home sometime in April 1776.

Angered and distraught by the continued bloodshed, by Parliament's interdiction of all trade with the colonies, and by apparent inaction and indecision, Americans grew more radical. In January 1776 Thomas Paine's *Common Sense* ignited this powderkeg. This brilliant polemic argued with persuasive simplicity that George III was a "Royal Brute," that it was ludicrous for a continent to be ruled by an island, that Americans had quite simply to choose between submission to abject tyranny and liberty and self-rule. In May the Virginia Convention formally declared independence, and the Congress sent an urgent request asking the colonies to set up independent governments. By July 4, 1776, Congress had adopted the Declaration of Independence.

Thomas Marshall had been appointed a major in the Continental army during the occupation of Norfolk. In July 1776 John Marshall followed his father into the Continental army, once more as a first lieutenant. While Thomas Jefferson and George Mason were, respectively, drafting the Declaration of Independence and the Virginia Declaration of Rights, two of the most important state papers of the American Revolution,

John Marshall associated "with brave men from different
states who were risking life and everything valuable in a common cause believed by all to be most precious."

The Continental army was scarcely an army at all—nondescript, half militia, half regular, ill-trained, ill-equipped,
and, for the most part, ill-led. With its numbers constantly
fluctuating because of desertions and resignations, it had
fought in desultory fashion since the summer of 1775 without
victories except, perhaps, for the psychological boost from
the storied battle of Trenton. Washington had then crossed
the frozen Delaware River on Christmas Eve with a small
force—Thomas Marshall among them—to defeat an even
smaller and largely drunken enemy force. It was an army,
said John Marshall, "decidedly inferior, not only in numbers,
but in every military requisite except courage."

Many difficulties resulted from the decision by Congress
to share responsibility with the states. The states appointed
colonels and lesser officers; Congress appointed the higher
officers. Each regiment came from a specific state, which was
responsible for keeping it filled with enlistments. This
arrangement produced nearly insurmountable problems;
and, in one form or another, this federalism pursued Marshall through the army and his career as statesman and
chief justice.

The various colonies had sought independence individually; they had, in fact, declared it that way. The Continental
Congress represented a union of colonial causes, not a national will. The states were intensely jealous of their own interests and of each other. Congress was inefficient, although
it performed better than might have been expected. Those,
like Marshall, who "partook largely of the sufferings and feelings of the army" did not, however, have the advantage of
hindsight. Campaigning with armies, experiencing the tedium
and unrelieved boredom of daily camp life, and witnessing
the social and economic dislocation produced by the War for
Independence affected Marshall. The army took him outside

Virginia, indelibly fixed his attitudes on government and society, and established personal ties useful and comforting in
later years. For the remainder of his life he was devoted not
only to Union but to a government competent to its preservation. "I was confirmed," he said, "in the habit of considering
America as my country, and congress as my government."

Marshall gained enough army experience to sustain those
impressions. He had been commissioned in July 1776, but not
until a march to Philadelphia for inoculation against smallpox
in January 1777 was he ordered to active duty. It was May
before his company joined the main army at Princeton, New
Jersey. He finally saw action in the battles at Brandywine
Creek and at Germantown, where he was wounded in the
hand. After that disappointing campaign drew to a close, he
settled with the army into winter quarters at Valley Forge,
some twenty miles outside Philadelphia. There, while the
British squandered the winter's opportunity to crush the beat-
en patriot army, he endured the hardships, the privations,
and the symbolic irony of the entire war—that patriots in the
field suffered more from the depredations of Americans than
they did from British tyranny.

At Valley Forge, John Marshall continued to display those
qualities first noticed that day on the muster field in May
1775. Popular, personable, and winsome, he had a remarkable
capacity "for leavening the dough of serious purpose with the
yeast of humor and diversion." When he was not urging his
comrades on to greater exertions or enlivening their gloom
"by his inexhaustible fund of anecdote," he was indulging his
lifelong passion for pitching quoits or running races. He was
called "Silverheels," after his habit of racing in stockings into
which his mother had stitched white heels.

Because eighteenth-century armies were microcosms of the
class-conscious, deferential societies they served, they were
practical schools of government similar in many respects to
experience in Virginia. Just prior to the encampment at Valley
Forge, Marshall had been appointed deputy judge advocate,

responsible for the prosecution of courts-martial. But justice at Valley Forge was more often done by stern disciplinary codes than through formal proceedings. Ordinary soldiers were summarily given one hundred lashes across the bare back for attempted desertion. Most of the deputy judge advocate's duties were notarial—taking affidavits, witnessing proceedings, and informally settling minor disputes. The job was analogous to that of the county court justice in Virginia. John Marshall had never served as justice of the peace, and his experience as deputy judge advocate compensated somewhat for what he had missed in Virginia.

At Valley Forge, Marshall began to revere George Washington as the symbol of the American cause, and he first met Alexander Hamilton, whose attitudes and opinions he respected and admired. He renewed his friendship with James Monroe, an old schoolmate from Campbell's academy, and that friendship survived later political hostility.

The spring of 1778 saw the army much improved. Congress had appointed the capable Nathanael Greene as quartermaster, and the stuffy Prussian drillmaster, Baron von Steuben, had polished the rough edges off the raw troops. In addition news came of the great victory at Saratoga that winter and of the French alliance—crucial to victory—that spring.

John Marshall saw action once more in June when the army engaged the British in 100° heat at Monmouth Courthouse. In that engagement he served with the light infantry, an elite corps handpicked for demonstrated bravery, agility, stamina, and determination. In July and August 1779 Marshall again joined the light infantry in the assaults on Stony Point and Paulus Hook along the Hudson River. After that, except for some small activity during Benedict Arnold's 1781 invasion of Virginia, he returned to private life.

By the autumn of 1779 John Marshall yearned to have done with the war which had dragged on interminably and had disrupted his family life and his career. Officers, Virginia gentlemen, were impoverished by their commissions. Increasingly, they felt that they were conferring rather than receiving favors in holding them. The war had devastated the Marshall family. Since February 1778 Thomas Marshall had been stationed at Yorktown in command of a Virginia artillery unit, and John's mother, brothers, and sisters had remained at the family estate at Oak Hill. John visited them in the autumn of 1778. When supper time arrived, his mother used the last of the flour to make a little bread. She had been saving the flour for just such a special occasion. Seeing the bread, the "little ones cried for some, and brother John inquired into matters," his sister recalled. "He would eat no more of the bread which could not be shared with us. He was greatly distressed at the straits to which the 'fortunes of war' had reduced us." No doubt this experience turned John Marshall's thoughts once again to his career.

The opportunity to act on this growing concern came in December 1779 when the Virginia Line was transferred to the defense of the Carolinas, and John Marshall was ordered back to Virginia to command such troops as the legislature would raise. Because the troops were never raised, he had an "inactive interval" to visit his father at Yorktown and, sometime before May 1, 1780, to study law twelve miles distant at the College of William and Mary at Williamsburg, the state capital and the seat of learning and of manners in Virginia. There he had the opportunity to observe state government in operation and to gain a familiarity with the men who made its institutions work. One of these was George Wythe—in many ways the personification of Virginia government.

As part of a general reorganization of William and Mary, Governor Thomas Jefferson had established a chair of Law and Police in December 1779. Wythe, who held that chair, was a self-made, prominent member of the gentry. He had served in the House of Burgesses; the Continental Congress, where he had been a signer of the Declaration of Independence; and the House of Delegates. In 1780 he was appointed a justice of the High Court of Chancery and the Court of

Appeals. This teacher, who numbered Jefferson among his students, was one of the most respected lawyers in Virginia and in the nation. Exposure to Wythe guaranteed exposure to higher, and more formal, if not final, institutions of government than was possible on the hustings and the county court.

Wythe's purpose as a teacher was to form leaders as well as lawyers. He expected his students to read and take notes from the English legal classics and from such law reports and collections of statutes as were available. Twice a week, he lectured—more on political theory than on legal substance and procedure—and questioned students on passages from their readings. Once or twice a month he had the students argue cases before him and other faculty members at a moot court in the old capitol building. Each Saturday the students gathered into model legislatures where, during the July 1780 term, they debated bills that Wythe and others drafted for the state legislature. In addition, Phi Beta Kappa, the national honor society founded in 1776, offered a chance through debate to develop and polish skills in public speaking.

Marshall participated fully in all these activities. He also attended lectures on natural philosophy that treated such topics as physics, chemistry, and astrology. In Phi Beta Kappa debates he joined Spencer Roane, later chief justice of Virginia, and Bushrod Washington, nephew of the commander in chief and later Marshall's colleague on the Supreme Court. In one of the moot courts Marshall led a team of four against another team led by William Short, founder of Phi Beta Kappa and later Jefferson's private secretary. Marshall's performance, according to Short, demonstrated no exceptional ability.

These three months were the full extent of John Marshall's formal training in the law, not an unusual course at the time. For Virginia gentlemen the law was a practical profession. Most lawyers learned their law while practicing it. Brief study was usually sufficient to men whose primary interests were farming, commerce, politics, and land speculation. Wythe himself was self-taught in the law, and Marshall's legal education was better than that of many of his countrymen who simply read under some country lawyer and were admitted to practice after a perfunctory examination.

Marshall's "Law Notes," over two hundred pages of notes on legal subjects arranged alphabetically but ending abruptly under "L," revealed an effort to set straight in his own mind the peculiar blend of English precedents and American adjustments known as the common law. The "Law Notes" also revealed the final step in the shaping of Marshall's career— marriage into a prominent Virginia family. In various places on the first page of that notebook he had written the name "Ambler," "Polly Ambler," only "Polly," or "Miss Maria Ambler." John Marshall and Mary Willis Ambler, called "Polly" all her life, spent nearly fifty years together. Marshall remained as steadfastly devoted to this union as to the political union of the states.

Mary Ambler was the second of four daughters of Jaquelin Ambler and Rebecca Burwell, the shy beauty who had rejected Jefferson for Ambler. Though reduced by war, the Amblers were one of Virginia's first families. Jaquelin Ambler was an educated, urbane businessman known throughout the capital for his social grace and good sense. In 1779 he was one of eight members of the Council of State, which the legislature periodically elected to advise the governor. He had moved his residence to Yorktown where he occupied a small tenement next door to the officers' quarters where Thomas Marshall was staying.

Colonel Marshall regularly acted as guardian to the Ambler girls during their father's trips to the capital. On these occasions he frequently read them letters from his eldest son and told them stories about the "gay-hearted young captain, who was called Silverheels." Years later Polly's older sister Eliza recalled that they had grown accustomed to hear John "spoken of by all as a very *paragon* . . . and every line received from him was read with rapture." When Thomas Marshall told the girls of his son's forthcoming visit, Eliza recalled that they were excited to the highest pitch and "were particularly emulous who should be first introduced." Polly astounded her sister and friends by announcing that they were worrying needlessly, that she, not yet fourteen and very shy and diffident, had "resolved to set her cap at him and eclipse us all."

When John Marshall arrived at Yorktown shortly after Christmas 1779, the girls, expecting "an Adonis," were disappointed in the tall, awkward countryman with unpolished manners whose only redeeming qualities were piercing black eyes and a winning smile. Polly was not disappointed. She knew that Marshall was an eminently likable human being. Beneath the careless dress and lack of polish "there dwelt a heart complete with every virtue." Marshall tells us he "formed a strong attachment" and spent a month watching the girls as his father had done, reading them poetry and works of the best authors, and no doubt explaining the vicissitudes besetting the Continental army and the patriot cause.

In June 1780 the Amblers moved to the new capital at Richmond, stopping on their way at Williamsburg, where a ball was held for the girls. Marshall spent much time wooing Polly. His attentions, he wrote, "though without any avowed purpose, nor so open or direct as to alarm, soon became ardent & assiduous." When he finished his schooling, he spent some time at Richmond at the Amblers' during the summer. Early in August he passed the bar examination, and Governor Jefferson issued his license to practice. On August 28, 1780, he was admitted to practice law in Fauquier County, 135 miles away from Richmond. That autumn he walked to Philadelphia—at the incredible pace of thirty to thirty-five miles a day—for another inoculation against smallpox, because Virginia law made it nearly impossible to obtain inoculation within the colony.

The Old Dominion had remained largely untouched by the war since conflicts with Dunmore at Great Bridge and Norfolk in 1775, but in 1781 British armies moved north from the Carolinas. Benedict Arnold sailed up the James River, attacking Richmond and neighboring towns and putting the government—including the Amblers and Governor Jefferson, whose lack of preparation and flight proved a mighty thorn of embarrassment in ensuing years—to flight. Marshall assumed command of a militia unit that ambushed a British raiding party and inflicted the only enemy casualties during the invasion. Arnold quickly retired, and, in October 1781, Washington and the French defeated General Charles Cornwallis at Yorktown and virtually ended the War for Independence. The problems of peace and the implications of independence—with which John Marshall would wrestle for the rest of his life—were still in the future for the young gentleman lawyer eager to practice, to marry, to rise in the world.

He had resigned his commission in February before Arnold's invasion but was unable to begin practicing until the courts reopened in October. In April 1782 Marshall was elected to the House of Delegates from Fauquier County. That duty took him to Richmond and to Polly. The new capital was the site of the state superior courts—no better place for the ambitious lawyer. Then, too, Richmond offered the opportunity to participate in state government and to gain entrance to the inner circle of influence. The Amblers were of that circle—Jaquelin had been elected state treasurer in 1782. In that household, John Marshall was already familiar.

At Richmond he renewed his courtship of Polly, who was by this time near the marrying age of sixteen. In addition to the usual "tiffs & makings up," Marshall had to contend with a rival suitor, Major Richard Anderson. Apparently eager to conclude his suit and get on with the business of his career, Marshall went to the Ambler home and proposed in direct and unequivocal fashion. Uncertain, confused, or simply playing the coquette, Polly refused, saying no when she meant yes. Disappointed and frustrated, the ardent young lover strode from the house and mounted his horse to ride off to

Fauquier County. Polly began to weep uncontrollably when she saw the harm done. At that point, her cousin snipped a lock of Polly's hair and rode after Marshall to offer this token as assurance that Polly had in fact meant to say yes. John Marshall, "supposing she had sent it," said his sister many years later, "renewed his suit and they were married." Polly Marshall wore a locket containing a snippet of hair the rest of her life. John wore the same locket after her death.

They married in the Hanover County home of Polly's cousin, John Ambler, on January 3, 1783. John Marshall was twenty-seven; Polly a few months shy of seventeen. As a lawyer, war hero, son of a prominent Virginian, member of the House of Delegates, and propitiously married, John Marshall was ready to make his mark and take his place in Virginia.

I I

Richmond Lawyer

1783–1788

To PLAN A CAREER is one thing. To realize it grand-
ly is quite another. John Marshall plunged headlong into the
land, the law, and the politics of Virginia. He had greater
ambitions than to remain a county lawyer and spend his time
in an unexciting and not too lucrative practice before the
county courts, in the management of his lands in Fauquier
County, and in dilatory attendance at the House of Delegates.
He revealed the extent of those intentions when he moved to
Richmond. The state capital was as fraught with danger as
it was loaded with opportunity. In addition to the higher cost
of living, a young lawyer with little money had to overcome
the formidable obstacle of competition with the talented and
well-established lawyers at the Richmond bar. The profusion
of important persons at the capital rendered family connections less important there than in Fauquier County. Success
at Richmond demanded assiduous cultivation and hard work,
and Marshall succeeded. Within three years of his marriage
he was a leading member of the Richmond bar. By 1788,
when he participated in the Virginia Convention to ratify the
new federal Constitution, he was probably unsurpassed in
knowledge of the state's law and courts.

During these years of great ferment Virginia and the
nation wrestled with the pressing problems of finance, of
interstate harmony, and of liberty. Marshall's personal and

professional involvement with the struggle to revise the Virginia constitution, with veterans' pay, with Kentucky lands, with depreciating currency, with taxes, and with British debts forced him inescapably to think about power and its allocation. Each year he grew more dissatisfied. Virginia was his prime concern, but it became clear to Marshall, as to James Madison, that only an invigorated federal government could adequately protect the state's interests. The constitutional principles which Marshall later pronounced on the Supreme Court received intellectual form from his Richmond experience.

*   *   *

Service in the legislature was necessary for an ambitious lawyer. The lower house did not pay well—its members received only small per diem allowances. But it did count among its members many of the judges of the superior courts and important Richmond lawyers. A demonstration of hard work and ability helped a budding career along.

Richmond was a raw town, a far cry from the dignified and refined old Williamsburg. With its sprawling, nondescript frame houses, the town reminded one traveler of an Arabian village, with saddled horses at every turn and swarms of flies and riders in the few muddy streets. The only building large enough to accommodate the legislature was an abandoned warehouse, untouched when the British had burned the city during Arnold's 1781 invasion and now the scene of every public function from balls to banquets.

Delegates to the House took lodging wherever they could find it. Most of them wound up crammed into the only tavern, run by a Neopolitan named Formicola. Two enormous upstairs rooms served as a kind of barracks where delegates slept in beds placed side by side. The downstairs area was more congenial. Every evening "generals, colonels, captains, senators, assemblymen, judges, doctors, clerks, and crowds of gentlemen of every weight and caliber and every hue of dress, sat all together about the fire, drinking, smoking, singing, and talking ribaldry." The sociable, easy-going, disheveled John Marshall made many friends and established connections as he had at Valley Forge and Yorktown. When he and Polly moved to a two-room cottage behind the Ambler residence after their marriage, Marshall remained active in the social club at Formicola's—sounding opinion, catching rumors, winning influence.

Virginia politics in the 1780s remained oligarchical and deferential. Factions constantly realigned on issues and personalities but without firm ideological divisions. The Revolution had not changed the composition of the House. Giants of property and reputation such as George Mason and Edmund Randolph maintained their power by careful attention to detail and to demanding committee work. To advance, a young delegate had to win their approval. Every delegate was appointed to at least one of the great standing committees and some of the lesser ones, but most dissipated their energies at the tavern and gaming tables. Marshall served regularly on the Committee on Courts of Justice. He was also a member of the standing committees on Privileges and Elections and Propositions and Grievances and of numerous select committees appointed periodically to draft reports and legislation. By attending regularly and working diligently, he revealed his seriousness and won the approval of the inner circle.

During the fall session of 1782 the House elected Marshall to the Council of State. The Council was no longer the prestigious body it had been before the Revolution; although it was the executive branch of Virginia government, the state constitution had reduced that branch nearly to impotence.

The Council lacked distinction, but it had advantages. It met daily and paid its members on the basis of days attended. A diligent councilor had to reside in Richmond, an opportunity for a young lawyer without an established practice and with a small income. Election to the Council may have been critical to Marshall's decision to settle at Richmond.

The steady growth of Marshall's law practice after 1782 persuaded him to resign from the Council. Less dependent on political income, he felt greater demands on his time for his own business. Then in 1784 the courts ruled that a councilor could not practice law, and this opinion concerning "a Counsellor's standing at the bar," Marshall wrote, caused his resignation. Later that spring Marshall was again elected to the House of Delegates from Fauquier County. His residence in Richmond presented no problem, because Virginia law allowed candidates to seek office wherever they held land.

As a lawyer–politician, Marshall had a large personal and professional interest in Kentucky land. A boom had followed passage of the Virginia land law of 1779, which offered some warrants to veterans upon proof of military service and allowed the purchase of others with depreciated paper currency. The warrant was little more than a hunting license. The establishment of title to the land required a complicated series of steps involving the location and survey of a tract and the filing of papers with the Virginia land office at Richmond. Because Virginia had granted more land than was available and because surveying techniques were primitive, conflicting claims abounded. In such cases the only way to protect a claim was to file a caveat with the land office against a rival claim to the same parcel and then await a court decision. Every inch of Kentucky land was quickly disputed. Courts in Virginia— and in Kentucky after statehood in 1792—were clogged with lawsuits. A lawyer was much in demand, especially one who had been an officer in the Continental army, resided in Richmond, was close to the land office, had legislative connections, and was the son of the oldest and best established surveyor in Kentucky.

Thomas Marshall, who had been appointed surveyor of Fayette County, Kentucky, in 1781 and had moved there with his family in 1783, formed a partnership typical for the time with his lawyer–son in Richmond. After John Marshall had obtained the warrants, Thomas would survey the land—and he knew the choicest parcels. John would then file the papers with the land office. The two men were well situated also to obtain warrants and file caveats for other claimants and to speculate in depreciated warrants. By the time the boom had crested in 1784, the Marshalls between them owned Kentucky lands in the tens of thousands of acres. Hardly a statesman in Virginia was not similarly involved. "I have been maneuvering amazingly," Marshall wrote to his close friend James Monroe in 1784, "to turn your warrants into cash. If I succeed I shall consider myself a first rate speculator."

In addition to assisting with veterans' land claims, Marshall devoted much time to obtaining pensions from Virginia and from the Congress. "They knew," he said, "that I felt their wrongs and sympathized in their sufferings, and had partaken of their labors, and that I vindicated their claims upon their country with a warm and constant earnestness." Veteran or not though, clients discovered that Marshall won cases. It was not his gangling appearance and disheveled attire that impressed them, but his knack for going to the heart of issues. He was a good lawyer.

By November 1784 he was sufficiently established and confident of his prospects to join with some other Richmond lawyers in an advertisement informing the public that they would henceforth not "undertake any cause after the 1st day of January next, without the fee and the tax of the writ in hand." He had come a long way since 1782.

"Lawyers are plants that will grow in any soil that is cultivated by the hands of others," wrote Hector St. John de Crevecoeur in 1782. "The fortunes they daily acquire in every province, from the misfortunes of their fellow citizens, are surprising." Lawyers, as Marshall demonstrated, were eager entrepreneurs; and post-revolutionary hard times generated litigation. A shortage of money hindered repayment of Virginia's war debt and produced a running battle over taxation, debts to British creditors, and court reorganization. John Marshall grew frustrated at the legislature's failure to address these problems. In the 1784 sessions, "Not a bill of public importance, in which an individual was not particularly interested has passed," he lamented to Monroe. Nearly every measure he had supported had met either defeat or postponement. Such had been the fate of a proposal to increase the tax rate and to encourage intermarriage between Indians and whites. "Our prejudices," he said, "oppose themselves to our interests & operate too powerfully for them."

Anti-British sentiment and an understandable reluctance to pay the enemy had induced Virginia in 1777 to legislate that debts owed British creditors could be paid into the state treasury. The Treaty of Paris, which ended the war in 1783, had explicitly obliged the states to remove such legislation. The House of Delegates instead passed a resolution tying repayment to British reparation for slaves removed during the war and to evacuation of military posts on the western frontier. Marshall, disturbed by this policy, believed it to be another example of the erosion of the sanctity of contracts and public virtue, and he felt that such erosion threatened anarchy and confusion.

Court reorganization was part of a general revision of the laws that Jefferson and Madison had pushed with only moderate success since 1779. The glut of litigation had created a litigant's hell and a lawyer's paradise, but the great number of cases exhausted the lawyers who struggled to litigate them. Lengthy dockets in the state courts, centralized at Richmond, delayed cases and raised costs, putting litigation beyond the means of a great many people. Yet the county courts were helpless, because complex legal questions were beyond the competence of the lay judges. A committee on which Marshall served drafted legislation establishing circuit courts to alleviate the congestion at Richmond and furnish professional judges for trials in the counties. Justices of the peace and

"County Court lawyers" defeated the legislation, however. Marshall blasted the selfishness of parties opposed to "every Measure which may expedite & facilitate the business of recovering debts & compelling a strict compliance with contracts."

Marshall remained active in public life, although he did not stand for election to the House again until 1787. In July 1785 the Richmond voters chose him to fill a seat on the city's governing body, the Common Hall. Further testimony to his popularity and professional reputation came several days later when he was chosen city recorder and member of the Richmond City Hustings Court. These positions offered Marshall an excellent vantage point from which to observe city government and enhance his career. As city recorder he kept records and was responsible for prosecuting actions for the municipality.

In April 1785 Marshall was admitted to practice before the Court of Appeals and could look forward to a lucrative income from the important clients before that tribunal. His legal reputation rested on his ability as an appellate lawyer. Frequently in closing arguments his ability to seize the important issues, to penetrate the heart of the controversy, and his compelling logic served both himself and his clients well. After 1785 most of his practice was before the Court of Appeals. Ultimately he argued over one hundred cases there through the 1790s.

His first argument in *Hite* v. *Fairfax* in May 1786 marked the beginning of a lifelong personal and professional involvement with the Fairfax lands. The case arose from a dispute over title to a portion of the Fairfax grant. Since 1749 it had been pending before the General Court, which in 1771 decided against the Fairfax title. Both parties appealed this decision, and, after the Revolution, the appeal lodged in the Virginia Court of Appeals. That court affirmed the General Court decision on May 6, 1786. Marshall and John Blake had represented the Fairfax interest; Edmund Randolph, then attorney general of Virginia, and John Taylor had argued for Hite's associates.

Personal knowledge of the land and the litigation aided Marshall when he delivered the closing argument. The Marshall lands in Fauquier County, on which he had grown up and which his father had deeded to him in 1785, derived from the Fairfax title. His father had been a surveyor for Fairfax and for a commission appointed by the General Court in 1769. To John Marshall the challenge to the validity of the entire Fairfax title was another disturbing symptom of the times. Virginia had been moving for some time to sequester land held by aliens, an injustice not only to Fairfax and his heirs but to all who held under some Fairfax title. Bypassing the narrow questions of the immediate case, Marshall focused his argument on the validity of the Fairfax title. The wisdom of such grants was not a matter for judicial inquiry—a point he would make again and again throughout his judicial career. The grant itself was the important issue, and Marshall argued that there could be no doubt about its validity, "for if he have not title, he could convey none." Although the court decided for Hite in the particular case, it established the validity of the remainder of the Fairfax title. The decision, then, "served as a spur to further claims predicated on Lord Fairfax's grants and was the beginning, rather than the end, of litigation over titles in the Northern Neck."

That summer Marshall ran unsuccessfully for attorney general, although he received a handsome vote. But Edmund Randolph, elected governor, notified his clients that he was turning his practice, one of the largest in the capital, over to John Marshall.

Not all Marshall's time was devoted to serious matters. Richmond had a busy social life, especially during legislative sessions, and he could devote time and money to any of numerous activities. He was an enthusiastic member of the Jockey Club, which organized the horse races at Broad Rock track every May and October. During the winter months the Richmond Assemblies organized social activities every other week at the Eagle Tavern. Marshall was one of the original subscribers to the Richmond Circulating Library. He was an active Mason. He was a member of the Society of the Cincinnati, an organization of veteran officers of the Continental army, and of the Society of St. Taminy, which held dances in Indian costumes twice yearly. Regular meetings of the social club at Formicola's and an endless round of dinners, card games, and quoits filled out the days.

Home was a sanctuary offering the greatest peace and happiness a man could know in this life. Polly was his quiet but important partner. She, too, participated in the balls and banquets and even in the card games that so delighted the Richmond ladies, but she retained her early shyness. That "timidity so influenced her manners," Marshall wrote after her death in 1831, "that I could rarely prevail on her to display in company the talents I knew her to possess. They were reserved for her husband & her select friends." Serious and gentle in her deportment, "she possessed a good deal of chaste, delicate & playful wit, and, if she permitted herself to indulge this talent, told her little story with grace, & could mimic very successfully the peculiarities of the person who was the subject." Polly Marshall bore ten children between 1784 and 1805, six of whom lived to maturity.

Misfortune struck the Marshalls cruelly in 1786. Their second child died five days after its birth in June, and, after the miscarriage of another pregnancy several months later, Polly suffered a nervous breakdown from which she never fully recovered. "Mrs. Marshall . . . is Insane," wrote Jefferson's daughter; "the loss of two Children is thought to have Occasioned it." Marshall's account book recorded the hiring of servants to perform household tasks, and he did the family marketing the remainder of his life. Noise of any kind disturbed Polly sorely. Many stories survive of Marshall moving his law office to an outbuilding, quieting the grandchildren in later years, rising at night to still noisy neighborhood animals, walking in his slippers, and even asking the city fathers not to ring bells for fear of disturbing Polly. Yet his devotion remained constant and even deepened. For the next forty-five years he was always eager to return to Richmond and to his "most desirable & agreeable companion," whose talents "beguiled many of those winter evenings when her protracted ill health & her feeble nervous system, confined us entirely to each other."

Events in 1786 also cast a pall over the nation. "The state of the Confederacy," Marshall wrote, was "a subject of deep solicitude to our statesmen." Many concluded with George Washington that there was grave cause for alarm. When a single state could block efforts at solving the persistent problems of commerce and revenue, as Rhode Island had done in 1783 and as New York did in 1786, the only hope for improvement lay with reforming the Articles of Confederation to provide an energetic and pervasive national government. The convention at Annapolis, Maryland, had met to discuss these concerns in September 1786, recommending that all the states appoint commissioners to meet in Philadelphia in May 1787 to devise "such changes as shall appear to them necessary to render the constitution of the federal government adequate to the exigencies of the Union." Shays's Rebellion, a tax revolt in Massachusetts in September, galvanized sentiment for the reform. Within a year a new constitution had been drafted and submitted to the Congress and the states for ratification.

Marshall could not escape involvement. Politics was a staple in the conversational diet of Richmond, and at the tables at which Marshall dined nearly all supported some enlargement of the federal government. His close friend James Monroe had worked diligently but unavailingly to that end while serving as a delegate to the Confederation Congress from 1783 to 1786. James Madison, with whom Marshall had served in the legislature in 1784, was the "parent" of both the Annapolis and Philadelphia conventions. Randolph had also been prominent, as had Washington, whom Marshall already called "the greatest Man on earth."

As a legislator and lawyer, Marshall had witnessed Virginia's insouciance to the will of Congress on questions of British debts and sequestration of British property. He had grown anxious over the strength of movements to suspend tax collection, to delay legal proceedings, to abrogate contracts. The "faith of a nation, or of a private man," he wrote later, "was deemed a sacred pledge, the violation of which was equally forbidden by the principles of moral justice, and of sound policy." After 1784 Madison had led the opposition to these measures, and Marshall supported him not from personal allegiance but from conviction. Ideology was beginning to replace personality in Virginia politics.

Shays's Rebellion confirmed Marshall's worst fears. Farmers and debtors in western Massachusetts, plagued by excessive farm interest rates and the prospect of imprisonment for back debts and taxes, forcibly closed the county courts to prevent further judgment. Marshall could not condone their methods. Individual distress, he believed, should be relieved only by frugality and industry and not by a relaxation of the laws. These "bloody, dissentions," he wrote, "cast a deep shade over that bright prospect which the revolution in America and the establishment of our free governments had opened to the votaries of liberty throughout the globe." He feared that man might prove incapable of self-government and that another revolution impended. His pessimism expressed the attitudes of a Virginia gentleman who believed in representative government, not in direct government by the people, and who was worried lest the Revolution had unleashed forces that threatened to destroy it.

Marshall believed in a "well-regulated democracy," in sovereignty lodged in but never exercised by the people. During the struggle for independence he had been an ardent champion of the self-government he had known to work well in

Virginia. His army experience and other "causal circumstances," especially "the general tendency of state politics," had dampened his enthusiasm. Experience taught him that he had formed too good an opinion of human nature and "that the many as often as the few, can abuse power, and trample on the weak, without perceiving that they are tyrants."

Many shared his view. Thomas Jefferson's *Notes on Virginia* had bemoaned the absence of separation of powers in Virginia after the Revolution and had warned about the dangers of "elected despotism." Madison early in 1787 had written a comprehensive critique of the Confederation pointing out that the "Vices of the Political System of the United States" were too little power in the Confederation and too much concentrated and unchecked power in the individual state legislatures.

General reform was indeed the purpose of the Philadelphia Convention. Madison proposed a unitary state that would have eliminated altogether the political power of the states. Compromises during that hot summer produced some modification and some allowance for shared power, but the Constitution which emerged in September still reflected the belief that only a new continental republic could save America's experiment. The new Constitution was to be the "supreme law of the land." It contained appropriate checks on potential abuses, but its attractiveness lay first of all in the redistribution of political power. Marshall, for one, "gave a high value . . . to that article in the constitution which imposes restrictions on the states."

The revolutionary implications of the new Constitution evoked a campaign to prevent ratification by the necessary nine states. The opposition hoped to call a second convention that would not go beyond necessary amendments to the Articles. Paradoxically, Virginia, which had taken the lead in promoting the Convention, assumed the lead in opposing its product. Two of her delegates to the Convention, the young governor Randolph and the able George Mason, had refused to sign the document; and Richard Henry Lee, one of the state's ablest politicians, began in October to pen the most distinguished of opposition, or antifederal, tracts—the "Letters of a Federal Farmer."

Yet Virginia's approval was crucial, and Marshall played a prominent part in the struggle for ratification. As a member of the House of Delegates, he proved himself "a determined advocate" for the Constitution. He framed the call for a convention to consider the document in terms acceptable to both its supporters and opponents.

Patrick Henry was the great threat to ratification in Virginia. It was bad enough that Henry was unsurpassed in oratory and dissimulation. Worse in 1787 was his immense potential influence in Kentucky. Two issues agitated that mecca of Virginia land speculators: statehood and trade on the Mississippi River. Virginia had supported statehood, but the Confederation Congress had dragged its feet and had also voted to sacrifice free navigation of the Mississippi in return for Spanish trade concessions that benefited northeastern merchants. Henry took both actions as evidence of the intent of northern states to frustrate southern expansion.

Kentucky was also Marshall territory, where father and son both had extensive landholdings and influence. In 1787 the Kentucky Convention to plan statehood had appointed John Marshall agent to present their proposals to the Virginia legislature, and Thomas Marshall represented a Kentucky district in the House of Delegates. The two were no match for Henry's constant agitation of the Mississippi question through 1787–1788. The "unceasing efforts of the enemies of the constitution made a deep impression" and turned a great majority against the Constitution.

Virginia had not witnessed such animated political discussion since the Revolution. As the March elections for convention delegates approached, both sides worked feverishly to win converts. Newspapers printed lengthy arguments—numbers of *The Federalist* essays supporting the Constitution among them—and debating societies packed houses for hours of extended, often heated argument. "The press teemed with the productions of temperate reason, of genius, and of passion," Marshall recalled, "and it was apparent that by each party, power, sovereignty, liberty, peace, and security; things most dear to the human heart, were believed to be staked on the question depending before the public."

The elections appeared to give supporters of the Constitution a slight edge, but both sides knew that the convention debates would be crucial. Madison believed the issue would be decided by about twenty-five delegates who, like Randolph, generally approved the plan for a stronger union but desired amendments to protect the rights of the people and of the states. About eighty, including Marshall, favored ratification without amendment, and sixty-odd opposed. Madison worried that Henry's oratory might persuade delegates from the wavering middle, especially the fourteen Kentucky delegates, to vote no. Washington's reputation and known support of the Constitution would win some support, even though he had chosen not to attend. Fortunately, Richard Henry Lee would be absent, depriving the opposition of his considerable talents.

National attention focused on Virginia as the 173 delegates made their way to Richmond for the opening of the convention on June 2. Eight states had already ratified, and Virginia's decision could determine the outcome in New York in mid-June. Public interest remained so keen that enough delegates were present to constitute a quorum the first day, and so many spectators crowded the capitol building that the delegates had to move to the new Academy Hall to accommodate the crowd.

Nowhere did the Constitution receive more thorough, more sophisticated, and more carefully reasoned exposition and discussion. Yet only twenty-three of the delegates spoke at all during the three-week session. Most prominent were Madison, Edmund Pendleton, Randolph (who was finally converted), Henry (Light Horse Harry) Lee, and George Nicholas, who spoke for the Constitution, and Mason and Henry, who spoke against it. The Constitutionalists acted in concert. The opposition could not, but Henry alone was more than a match. He dominated! Speaking on eighteen of the twenty-three days he tirelessly and masterfully conjured up a future with liberty destroyed by federal courts and a standing army and with western interests sacrificed to majority rule and northern indifference. He could, said Madison, undo in one word what had taken an hour to establish.

In all of this debate Marshall played an active part. But he was not an orator; he had never before given a major public address. His arguments began with "reluctance, hesitation, and vacancy of eye" and gradually grew stronger and more eloquent. He seemed in debate like "some great bird, which flounders on the earth for a while before it acquires impetus to sustain its soaring flight." He spoke on three occasions, in the first public reflections on the Constitution by a man who was to spend the last thirty-five years of his life expounding that document.

On the morning of June 10 thirty-two-year-old Marshall, tall, "slovenly dressed in loose summer apparel, with piercing black eyes," rose to deliver his first address; a rebuttal to Henry's attack on the taxing power of the proposed government. Marshall's loose, rambling address drew heavily upon the problems of Congress and the states during the Revolution to demonstrate that the gravest threats to liberty came not, as Henry had charged, from a consolidated government with a power to tax but from an ineffectual one, a "recommendation of anarchy." The only valid questions were whether the power given was necessary to the objects of the government and whether the power was sufficiently guarded. The new Constitution, he said, was designed to "secure and protect" liberty, not to endanger it, and the power to raise money, to tax, was indispensable to that object. The representative nature of the House of Representatives, without whose consent no tax could be levied, was a sufficient check. "The objects of your adoption," he told the delegates, "are Union, and safety against foreign enemies—Protection against faction—against what has been the destruction of all Republics."

Six days later in a short speech Marshall answered charges that the Constitution would deprive the states of control over their militias and establish that serious threat to liberty—a standing army. He demonstrated that both the states and the national government would have the same military powers they had enjoyed under the Confederation. The only restrictions laid upon the states were those in Article I, section 10 of the new Constitution, and that article expressly allowed the states to engage in war when invaded or in imminent danger. Fear of oppression was unnecessary. A government drawn from the people and answerable to them would not dare it. The unthinkable alternative was to risk liberty by allowing each state to fend for itself against foreign and domestic enemies. "United we are strong, divided we fall."

The nature of the Union loomed large in the last great debate over Article III, which established the federal judiciary. Henry, in particular, had attacked the judiciary from the beginning, exploiting popular fears about the threat of British debt collection and precarious titles to western lands. The hostility was not to courts in general, or even to a limited national tribunal, but to the broad jurisdiction of the proposed federal judiciary. Agreement among Virginians of every persuasion that judicial review enabled courts to act as guardians of individual liberty did not solve the problem of the federal judiciary.

On June 19 Mason delivered an extended criticism of the federal judiciary. He denounced the new system as the instrument for the destruction of the state courts and, ultimately, of state government. The vague, unspecific language of the Constitution pointed in his mind to a design for "one great national, consolidated government." The gravest danger was the broad grant of power allowing Congress to establish an unlimited number of inferior federal courts. He argued that these courts would cover the land, allowing British creditors to sue for their money, the Fairfax heirs to sue for their confiscated estate, and land companies outside Virginia to reassert the validity of their western claims. Adding still more gloom, he pointed to the expense of appeals and the absence of a provision for jury trial in federal courts. Henry reinforced Mason's points with his usual moving oratory. "The purse is gone, the sword is gone," he lamented, and now Virginia justice was to go as well.

Marshall replied point by point. On June 20, late in the afternoon, he delivered his ablest address to the convention. Six years' experience as a legislator, lawyer, and land speculator had given him an intimate familiarity with legal problems, legal procedures, and Virginia courts. He began by calling the federal judiciary a "great improvement" that would make it possible to decide controversies previously either not handled or handled improperly. Mason's charge that federal courts would usurp state power or prevent a fair trial simply had "no foundation." The supremacy clause did make the laws of the United States paramount, but Marshall denied any plenary grant of authority to the national government. Federal courts would prevent abuses. Congressional powers, he argued, were confined to those enumerated in the Constitution. If Congress "were to make a law not warranted by any of the powers enumerated, it would be considered by the judges an infringement of the constitution which they are to guard. They would not consider such a law as coming under their jurisdiction. They would declare it void."

Federal courts, in short, would behave exactly as Virginia courts had since the Revolution. Many of the convention delegates had been present with Marshall at the first session of the Virginia Court of Appeals in November 1782. That court had ruled that it was the court's obligation to declare void legislative acts it deemed unconstitutional. "Is it not necessary," Marshall asked, "that the federal courts should have cognizance of cases arising under the constitution, and the laws of the United States?" The whole purpose of courts was to prevent usurpation and bloodletting by providing for the peaceful settlement of disputes. "To what quarter will you look for protection from an infringement on the constitution?" he asked. If the judiciary is not given the power, there "is no other body that can afford such protection."

The federal courts would, Marshall suggested, ease the strain on the overburdened state tribunals. "Look at the dockets.—You will find them crowded with suits which the life of man will not see determined." It would not be wrong to carry some of these suits to other courts. The state tribunals would not lose jurisdiction in the cases they now handled. Nor did any language in the Constitution forbid jury trials, any more than had the Virginia constitution. Again and again Marshall made the point that where power was to be trusted and where there was no reason to abuse it, it was "as well to leave it undetermined as to fix it in the Constitution."

Marshall's speech disposed of the judiciary question; Madison wrote to Hamilton that the opposition had made less impression than he feared. But the strain of three weeks of debate was beginning to tell. Pressure for action and adjournment mounted. Constitutionalists precipitated a vote on ratification and won some uncommitted delegates on June 24 by admitting that the Constitution had defects but indicating that they would accept amendments so long as they were recommendatory and not conditional. The next day Randolph issued a final dramatic reminder before the convention of the real issue—"union or no union." In a vote of 88 to 80, the convention rejected the prior amendments, and then it voted 89 to 79 to ratify the Constitution. New Hampshire had ratified during the debates, so Virginia became the tenth state to approve. New York followed shortly.

The Virginia Convention was the climactic point of Marshall's early life. After the ratification of the Constitution, he thought the "great principles of public policy" secure and sought once more to return to private life and to devote his energies to his practice, his family, and Virginia. But the Constitution turned the world topsy-turvy. Each year after 1788 his vigorous nationalism drew Marshall willy-nilly into national prominence. The circumstances of his life and the life of the nation altered dramatically, but the ideas formed by his experiences in the years to 1788 and first expressed during the debates that June remained constant during the fierce partisan struggles of the 1790s.

III

Federalist

1789–1797

THE CONSTITUTION ESTABLISHED a government whose energy aroused sectional jealousies and provoked vicious partisan disputes. The formation of political parties excited widespread fear of the imminent collapse of the American experiment in self-government. Disagreements over Alexander Hamilton's financial policies after 1790 demonstrated that national policies, though affecting all, benefited some more than others and stimulated competition for national power and influence. And the French Revolution, even more than Hamilton's policies, profoundly altered political life in the United States after 1789.

The commitment to self-government generated fearfulness, intolerance, and suspicion. Convinced that republics were historically fragile, Americans of the 1790s scrutinized every policy and politician for signs of decay. Those in power saw themselves not as a party but as the embodiment of the nation, and they regarded opposition as the work of anarchists and traitors. Those out of power and seeking it retaliated in kind, calling their foes monarchists and aristocrats bent on subverting the Constitution.

Because Virginia quickly became the fountainhead of the opposition, John Marshall could not escape the political maelstrom. His ambitions did not extend beyond Virginia. Until June 1797, when he accepted appointment as envoy extraordinary to France, he stayed in Richmond, firmly but politely refusing repeated offers of national office. Even so, his devotion to Washington, his economic interest, and his conviction that energetic government afforded the best national security placed him among the steadily diminishing band of administration supporters in the opposition stronghold. Though he deprecated parties as the bane of good government, he quickly became their political boss in Virginia.

*   *   *

Nothing in the Virginia of 1788 suggested the cleavages of the next decade. Political parties, in the sense of continuing electoral organizations commanding voter identification, had never before existed. Virginia politics, based on personal popularity, common political principles, and a strong tradition of independent judgment on specific issues, discouraged anything more structured than shifting, informal alliances.

Cause for concern had arisen, however. Many who had voted for the Constitution and those who had voted against it continued to have misgivings about the new plan of government. James Madison believed these fears would stimulate renewed opposition in the House of Delegates, which was scheduled to convene in October. Patrick Henry had pledged to oppose the new government "in a constitutional way," and neither Madison nor Marshall would be at hand to counter him. As the session approached, Betsy Ambler's husband Edward Carrington, an informant to Madison and Washington, reported a "phrenzy" of hostility to the Constitution among the delegates assembling at Richmond. The House of Delegates unanimously passed laws providing for the election of representatives to the First Congress and for the election of presidential electors. Then Henry skillfully guided the majority hostile to the Constitution through a series of maneuvers to assure proper representation of Virginia interests to the national government. The election of Richard Henry Lee and William Grayson as Virginia's first senators was a major defeat for nationalists who had backed Madison. Finally, the Virginia House of Delegates sent resolutions to Congress and to other states asserting its desire for amendments and reiterating its opposition to the Constitution in its existing form.

John Marshall felt the impact of these setbacks. Unanimously invited to become a candidate for Richmond's seat in the House of Delegates, he served from 1789 through 1791. He "yielded to the general wish," he said, partly because he "found the hostility to the government so strong in the legislature as to require from its friends all the support they could give it" and partly because the courts and the legislature sat in the newly completed capitol building. He could, "without much inconvenience" to his practice, take part in debates which interested him. The same elections returned a sympathetic majority able to offset the influence of Patrick Henry.

Marshall, convinced that participation in the national government would seriously injure his private affairs, refused to run for Congress. As it turned out, he was not needed. The spirit of sincere compromise and dedication that prevailed during the First Congress relieved southern anxiety about domination by northern commercial interests. Passage of the Bill of Rights allayed lingering fears and forebodings. Impressed by this easing of tension, Madison wrote Washington that "the great bulk of the late opponents" was entirely at rest.

"It was indeed a Miracle," Washington reflected in early January 1790, "that there should have been so much unanimity, in points of such importance, among such a number of Citizens, so widely scattered, and so different in their habits." The progress of the new federal government justified considerable optimism. Congress, with impressive dispatch and harmony, had provided executive departments to assist the president, had established the federal judiciary, and had amended the Constitution. Washington tried to preserve the spirit of compromise by balancing the rival sectional giants, North and South, when appointing men of talent to national office. He placed great hope in that small circle of department heads soon to be labeled "the cabinet." Marshall, however, declined Washington's offer of a commission as the first attorney of the United States for the District of Virginia. He shared the president's optimism and was still concerned primarily with his practice.

The miracle was short lived. Treasury Secretary Alexander Hamilton's financial plans rekindled sectional animosities. Like most Americans, Hamilton recognized the necessity of tackling the national debt, that unpleasant legacy of the Revolution owed to foreign creditors, army veterans, and merchants who had received government securities promising payment at a future date. The debt stood at over $50 million, and state debts totaled another $25 million. In January 1790 Hamilton proposed a refunding at face value, assumption of the state debts by the nation, and import duties and excise taxes to provide funds for repayment. In December he recommended establishment of a Bank of the United States. Congressman Madison and even fast friends of the government in Virginia opposed funding at par, because the securities had never sold at face value. The plan would create a speculator class supporting the government out of self-interest. Irritation increased when northern speculators, who seemed to have advance information, suddenly began buying up all available securities in Virginia. Even so, Virginians accepted the move as necessary bitter medicine for a national illness.

Assumption, however, generated universal condemnation. Virginia had repaid most of its Revolutionary debt through the sale of public land and regarded the plan as an unnecessary financial burden that would benefit only what Thomas Jefferson called "the stock-jobbing herd" of speculators. Led by Madison, Congress repeatedly rejected assumption, and in June 1790 Hamilton's entire plan seemed in jeopardy. Then Secretary of State Jefferson worked out a compromise. With the promise of northern votes to locate the new national capital on the banks of the Potomac, two Virginia congressmen changed their votes, and assumption passed. Among prominent Virginians, including Carrington and Henry Lee, who later became stalwart Federalists, only John Marshall supported the revised bill—and not without reservations.

Inevitably, Patrick Henry took the lead in opposition. When the legislature convened in October 1790, his resolution condemning assumption as unconstitutional passed. A special committee drafted a remonstrance to Congress condemning the attempt "to erect, and concentrate, and perpetuate a large monied interest" that would prostrate "agriculture at the feet of commerce" and create a consolidated government "fatal to the existence of American liberty." Virginia had ratified the Constitution only after assurances that powers not granted to the federal government were reserved to the states, and the legislature could "find no clause in the constitution authorizing Congress to assume the debts of the states!" The remonstrance thus asserted the right of a state to challenge the constitutionality of a federal law and succinctly formulated the principle of strict interpretation of the Constitution that later became an integral part of the ideology of the Republican party. While questioning the wisdom and expediency of national policies, Marshall insistently denied the assertion of their unconstitutionality. He continued to defend the government according to his independent judgment, even while the political environment increasingly demanded party loyalty.

Early in 1791 Congress dismissed the constitutional objections of a Madison-led minority and easily passed the remainder of Hamilton's program—the bank and an excise tax on whiskey. Within the cabinet, Jefferson and Attorney General Edmund Randolph objected to the bank on the same grounds expressed in the 1790 remonstrance—the lack of a specific grant of power to Congress to incorporate. Hamilton argued that Congress had an implied power to act wherever the Constitution did not set specific limits. Washington signed the bill, and economic prosperity soon blunted protest even in Virginia. Former opponents of assumption, such as Henry Lee, rejoined the ranks of the friends of the government. Even Patrick Henry had a change of heart.

Once again Marshall "bid a final adieu to political life." He now withdrew from the legislature and settled into a life that mirrored his attachment to family and profession, his growing income and prominence, and his easygoing, convivial personality. In 1790 he built a comfortable, two-and-one-half-story brick house—with smaller buildings for the kitchen, slave quarters, and a law office—within a short walk of the capitol building. The new residence offered the advantage of proximity to the court, the homes of leading lawyers, and the family of his wife Polly. Until the 1830s lawyers and judges gathered at this house on one Sunday each month for Marshall's famous "lawyers' dinners." Professional rivalries and political differences melted away. From early afternoon to late evening as many as thirty-two visitors gathered in the spacious dining room. They sipped toddy, cognac, and Madeira; dined on mutton, turkey, side dishes, and blancmanges; and finished a day of pleasant joshing and easy camaraderie with wine and bowls of raisins, nuts, and oranges.

Every Saturday afternoon Marshall joined a small group of prominent professional and business men at Buchanan's Spring, a resort on the outskirts of the city, for the weekly meeting of the Quoit Club. The group was distinguished by its membership—only thirty, always including the governor, and by invitation only—and its solitary rule banning any discussion of business, politics, or religion. Bank officers, successful merchants, lawyers, and politicians devoted the day to eating, drinking, joshing, and quoits. On weekdays Marshall still enjoyed a glass and cards at the taverns, attended the theater, shopped for the family provisions, and cared devotedly for Polly and their growing tribe.

Jefferson wrote Madison in June 1792 that Hamilton had "expressed the strongest desire that Marshall should come into Congress from Richmond declaring that there is no man

in Virginia whom he wishes so much to see there." Jefferson
believed that Marshall wished such a post and concluded that
Hamilton had "plyed him with flattery & solicitation."

In the spring of 1792 the lingering opposition of the
congressional minority erupted into public controversy in the
pages of the *National Gazette,* a Philadelphia newspaper established by Philip Freneau. Not only had Jefferson employed
Freneau as a part-time translator in the State Department but
Madison wrote for the paper, criticizing Hamilton's policies.
Dismayed, Washington asked Jefferson to explain the purpose
of the opposition. Jefferson informed the president that the
"republican party" viewed these policies as part of a plan to
change the government to monarchy. Monarchists and a "corrupt squadron" of congressmen owning government securities were the majority supporting Hamilton, he argued, and
true Republicans sought only to halt this perversion of the
Constitution. Hamilton counterattacked through the *Gazette
of the United States* and worked to build support in Virginia.

As the first step to organize Treasury Department support
in Virginia, Hamilton wrote to Marshall's brother-in-law Edward Carrington, a veteran administration informant who
had served as a United States marshal since 1789. Hamilton,
who placed reliable men in key treasury posts in all the states,
had appointed him federal supervisor of revenue in 1791.
When Hamilton complained to Carrington in May 1792 that
Madison and Jefferson were leading a faction hostile to the
administration and "subversive to the principles of good government," he expected his agent to initiate countermeasures.
By midsummer 1793 an administration faction had formed
around financiers and speculators in Richmond. John Marshall was at its head.

Support for the administration came naturally to Marshall.
He and his father were among the most successful Virginia
land speculators and dabbled also in certificates of the "assumed" Virginia debt in 1791 and 1792. His law practice
involved him with Robert Morris of Philadelphia, the fore-

most financier and speculator in America and an advocate of centralized government. Marshall had represented Morris's Virginia interests since the late 1780s. And, in 1793, Morris, John Marshall, his brother James Markham Marshall, and one more of their brothers-in-law, Rawleigh Colston, formed a syndicate to purchase the remainder of the Fairfax estate. The success of this venture depended to a large extent upon the vigorous government Marshall championed. In 1792 Marshall also had been actively involved in chartering the Bank of Richmond. In 1793 Madison wrote Jefferson that "Marshall, who is at the head of the great purchase from Fairfax, has lately obtained pecuniary aid from the Bank [of the United States], or people connected with it. I think it is certain that he must have felt, in the amount of the purchase, an absolute dependence on the monied interest, which will explain him to every one that reflects, in the active character he is assuming."

Marshall's political preference, however, reflected his total social situation, his background in the Virginia lesser gentry, his Revolutionary experience, his career, and his family. He and his father were close friends of Washington, with whom they shared membership in the Society of the Cincinnati, a group open only to officers of the Continental army and their eldest male descendants and from whose ranks the administration drew many of its appointees and supporters. Thomas Marshall was a federal tax collector in Kentucky. Two of John's brothers-in-law were steadfast administration supporters there: Humphrey Marshall, one of the few Kentucky Federalists at the Virginia ratifying convention, was a United States senator; and Joseph H. Daveiss was a United States attorney and an avid supporter of Alexander Hamilton.

Above all else, John Marshall was a Virginian. His support, like the opposition, was equivocal in the early 1790s. He was an ardent nationalist, as were Madison, Jefferson, and Monroe. Political parties had not yet formed, and many prominent Virginians including Patrick Henry and Henry Lee, were still shifting political allegiance. The administration faction in Richmond, then, reflected traditional Virginia politics. Hamilton's policies did not provide a suitable issue to test political preference.

The issue around which parties began to form in mid-1793 was the French Revolution, and Madison's comment about Marshall's "active character" referred to defense of the administration's posture toward that event.

The French Revolution radically transformed American politics. In 1789 most Americans supported the outbreak of revolution in France as a peaceful extension of their own and eagerly followed its progress. "We were all strongly attached to France," wrote Marshall, adding, "I sincerely believed human liberty to depend in a great measure" on the revolution's success. By the winter of 1792, however, news that the French had deposed the king, proclaimed a republic, and declared war on all monarchies gave Marshall sober second thoughts. While most Americans celebrated madly, the anarchy, bloodshed, and terror sickened him. France lacked every essential for republican government, with no balanced constitution and no means to restrain the passions of the mob. A "well-regulated democracy" was requisite to "human liberty," but unbridled democracy was, like death, "only a dismal passport to a more dismal hereafter," as Congressman Fisher Ames said later.

The French declaration of war on England in February 1793 sharpened disagreement by raising an issue which vitally affected the future of the United States. That war, wrote Jefferson, "kindled and brought forward the two parties with an ardour which our own interests, could never excite." In April, acknowledging the weakness of the country, the economic ties to England, and the thorny problem of the 1778 Franco-American alliance, Washington proclaimed strict neutrality and sternly warned Americans against compromising actions. Though some Republicans protested against the anti-

French tone and complained that Washington had acted without consulting Congress, they reluctantly agreed that neutrality was in the best interests of the United States.

The activities of the new minister of the French Republic, Citizen Edmond Charles Genêt, soon created popular frenzy and fundamentally altered American politics. When the new French government dispatched Genêt to America in 1793, warm, enthusiastic crowds greeted him at Charleston, South Carolina, and along his way to Philadelphia. Misled by the public adulation, this impetuous and overzealous young diplomat defied American neutrality by fitting out privateers in American ports to prey upon British shipping. When the government ordered him to cease these violations, Genêt foolishly demanded that Washington summon a special session of Congress to allow the people to judge his actions. Exasperated at this effrontery, the cabinet unanimously agreed to demand his recall. Partiality to France, Marshall said, would not render one "insensible to the danger of permitting a foreign minister to mingle himself in management of our affairs, and to intrude himself between our government and people."

Hamilton immediately sought to force a full presidential disclosure of Genêt's indiscretions by a display of public feeling. Accordingly, he judiciously leaked word to the press of Genêt's threatened appeal to the people. Then, in close collaboration with Chief Justice John Jay, Senator Rufus King of New York, and his network in the states, Hamilton carefully staged meetings of indignation to pass resolutions praising Washington, approving neutrality, and protesting bitterly against the French envoy. John Marshall organized the most successful and widely publicized of these meetings at Richmond on August 17. George Wythe presided over the adoption of resolutions "expressing our strong disapprobation of the irregular conduct of Mr. Genêt, our decided sense of the danger of foreign influence, and our warm approbation of the proclamation of neutrality." Like all the others, this meeting adjourned after adopting a memorial praising Washington for his past services and his devotion to peace. Marshall had drafted the resolutions and the memorial.

Madison attributed this coup to a "Philadelphia cabal," and the mortified Republicans staged counteroffensive meetings to correct any wrong impressions of Virginia sentiment. Their resolutions disowned Genêt without mentioning his name and affirmed loyalty to Washington, but they attributed the anti-French propaganda to partisans of Britain and monarchy, enemies of the Constitution. Monroe directed this countermove and repeated these charges in four articles published in the Richmond press through the fall of 1793 under the pseudonym "Agricola." Writing as "Aristides" and "Gracchus," Marshall penned four replies to his old friend.

Not since the Revolution had popular participation in politics been so great. The Genêt debates, by forcing sustained and organized efforts to guide and express public sentiment on a national issue, pushed the development of political parties. Both factions had taken steps which in two years would transform them into the Federalist and Republican parties. And Marshall, whatever his previous intentions, was now actively partisan in politics. "Seriously," he wrote a friend in March 1794, "there appears to me every day to be more folly, envy, malice, and damn rascality in the world than there was the day before and I do verily think that plain downright honesty and unintriguing integrity will be kicked out of doors."

A crisis with England quickened party conflict. In January 1794 Madison led congressional Republicans in a drive for discriminatory legislation against Britain. Partisan debate on this matter coincided with news of British depredations on American shipping and threats of Indian attacks along the Canadian frontier. Hoping to avoid the risks of war and coercive legislation, Washington sent John Jay to London to negotiate a settlement. Republicans, who regarded the appointment as further evidence of the influence of a pro-British faction, had little hope of an acceptable treaty. Jay's treaty, signed in late 1794, did not reach the United States until after Congress had adjourned in March 1795, and Washington kept its contents a close secret until he submitted it for ratification to a special session of the Senate in June. The secrecy heightened Republican fears that the treaty would accord with their expectations.

Meanwhile both Hamilton's decision to retire from the cabinet and the Whiskey Rebellion in the summer of 1794 were disturbing evidence of the unbridled democracy Marshall feared. He was particularly conscious of the threat of lawlessness: Kentucky mobs had burned Thomas Marshall in effigy and had assaulted his deputies. When Washington announced the uprisings as the work of democratic societies, Republicans concluded that the president too was now a tool of party.

These altercations weakened John Marshall's determination to stay out of the legislature to which he was elected once more in April 1795. He went to the polls to cast his ballot for a friend, but when the election began, someone put forward his name. Surprised at this "entirely unexpected proposition," he dissented decidedly, and after voting for his friend, spent the remainder of the day tending business at court. In his absence, he was elected. "I regretted this," he said, "for the sake of my friend. In other respects I was well satisfied at being again in the assembly." His services were sorely needed.

Before the Senate ratified Jay's treaty a Virginia senator leaked its provisions to the press. Immediately a wave of indignation swept the country. Republicans organized protest meetings urging the Senate to reject the treaty for its failure to settle either long-standing grievances or immediate problems. This time they asked Wythe to chair the Richmond meeting. The treaty had accomplished little beyond avoiding war, and it displeased even those who supported it. Washington, with grave misgivings, finally signed it in August 1795. Virginia was particularly agitated by the failure to provide

British compensation for slaves carried off during the Revolution, by the recognition of British land titles in the United States, and by the stipulation that the government would guarantee payment of debts to British creditors.

Furthermore, a constitutional question provoked continuing controversy. The treaty specifically limited the powers of Congress in certain commercial matters, and Republicans questioned whether the president could negotiate and approve such a compact. Noting that the Constitution did not require House approval of treaties, Jefferson wrote Madison that the entire business was simply a bold "party-stroke." Federalists, having lost their majority in the House, were attempting to "make law" through the Senate and the executive, "under color of a treaty" which would forever bind Republicans to favorable commercial ties to monarchical English interests.

A way out was apparent. Jay's treaty had also set up special commissions and required Congress to appropriate the funds to put those commissions in operation. Republicans planned to nullify the treaty by blocking those appropriations when the Congress convened in December 1795. Meantime they continued the war against the treaty in the Virginia legislature.

Within a week after the opening of the House of Delegates in November 1795, Republicans introduced a resolution commending Virginia's senators for their vote against ratification. The ensuing debate ranged over the entire treaty but focused on the charge of unconstitutionality. Appalled at the implicit censure of Washington, Marshall led the Federalists in determined but unsuccessful opposition. The resolution passed overwhelmingly. Only by dogged persistence did Federalists obtain an amendment exempting Washington from any censure.

Anticipating the Republican attack, Marshall had carefully studied all the opposition tracts and was "fully prepared" to demolish the charge of unconstitutionality. In an artful blend of detailed constitutional interpretation and adroit maneuvering, he argued that a treaty was valid when ratified by the president with the approval of the Senate and admitted the constitutional right of the House of Representatives to refuse appropriations—a point Federalists in Congress were unwilling to concede. The House, he argued, and not the Virginia legislature, was the proper forum for a discussion of constitutional objections.

Marshall's argument circulated widely. Federalist leaders in Congress, delighted to discover "a Virginian who supported with any sort of reputation the measures of the government," received him warmly when he visited Philadelphia in February 1796 to argue the case of the British debtors before the Supreme Court. Marshall's ability impressed Jefferson, too. Party strife had driven a firm wedge between these two kinsmen. Jefferson was relieved that Marshall had thrown off "the mask of Republicanism" long sustained by his "lax and lounging manners" and had "come forth in the plenitude of his English principles."

Marshall was not so much defending the treaty as the wise and vigorous government of Washington. It was true that the treaty would benefit the commercial interests among whom Marshall had clients. Moreover recognition of British land titles would assist the Marshall syndicate in its pursuit of the Fairfax estate. But more important, in the hanged, burned, and guillotined effigies of Hamilton, Jay, and Washington, Marshall saw the "fervour of democracy." Not even a statesman could render judgment on the merits of so complicated a treaty without "deep reflection in the quiet of his closet, aided by considerable inquiry." His response to the hasty and universal condemnations was "astonishment, mingled with humiliation, at perceiving such proofs of the deplorable fallibility of human reason." Republicans, he concluded, were "apostles of anarchy, not of freedom; and were consequently not the friends of real and rational liberty." Now that even Washington was the object of "atrocious calumny," Marshall increasingly identified Republicans with the excesses of revolutionary France and felt that the order, stability, and good government the Constitution had promised were in jeopardy.

Virginia Republicans believed that another wave of popular indignation would strengthen their effort to nullify the treaty in Congress. The legislature therefore passed and circulated a number of proposed constitutional amendments. The most significant was a proposal that no treaty "containing stipulations upon the subject of powers vested in Congress" could become law without the approval of a majority of the House of Representatives. These resolutions provided a convenient method of obtaining a national review of Virginia Republican complaints. No sooner had Washington submitted the treaty than Republicans demanded that he surrender to the House all the instructions and correspondence relating to Jay's negotiations. Debate over the demand and Washington's peremptory refusal, which consumed March and April 1796, once more placed a demand on Marshall's talents.

That spring Federalists started another campaign of meetings and resolutions to rouse popular approval of the treaty and of the president's refusal to release the Jay papers. Marshall led the Virginia Federalists in a complete surprise and rout of the Republicans. At a Richmond meeting in April he persuaded a "decided majority" to adopt resolutions declaring that the "welfare & honor of the nation required us to give full effect to the treaty negotiated with Britain." Alarmed and outmaneuvered, Republicans abandoned hope of political profit from Jay's treaty, and the House approved the appropriations by a narrow margin.

The biting partisanship of the treaty fight was a prologue to the bitter party contest for the presidency in 1796. Washington's retirement forced Federalists to plan carefully, particularly in the South, where John Adams was universally disliked and mistrusted. Nevertheless, Virginia was one of eight states that chose presidential electors through popular election; and campaigning in the centers of Federalist strength in Richmond, the Northern Neck, and the Shenandoah Valley netted one Adams elector—significant because only three electoral votes were the margin of victory.

The law practice that Marshall had so carefully cultivated since 1782 continued to grow and prosper through 1796. Most of his cases involved property disputes before the Superior Court of Virginia, the most important being *Ware* v. *Hylton* (1796), or the "Great British Debts Case." The establishment of federal courts in 1789 had provided those creditors a tribunal in which to press their claims, and they rushed to exploit it. A number of such cases were heard in the federal circuit court at Richmond after 1791. Marshall joined Patrick Henry, James Innes, and Alexander Campbell in defense of the debtors. An observer reported that "Marshall, it was acknowledged on all hands, excelled himself in *sound sense* and *argument*, which you know is saying an immensity." When the court decided for the debtors, the case was appealed to the United States Supreme Court. On February 2, 1795, Marshall had been admitted to practice before the Supreme Court; one year later he argued his only case before that tribunal. The Court struck down Virginia's sequestration law as contrary to the treaty of 1783. The decision injured Marshall's professional pride but soothed his conscience. He could not look disfavorably upon a federal court doing what he had hoped in 1788 it would do—upholding national law and the sacred obligation of contracts.

Federalist leaders in the capital were already celebrating Marshall's Virginia defense of Jay's treaty. "His head," commented Rufus King, "is one of the best organized of anyone that I have known." A French observer, Duc François de La Rochefoucauld-Liancourt, remarked on Marshall's ability and then noted that he had refused "several employments under the general government, preferring the income derived from his professional labours (which is more than sufficient for his moderate system of economy), together with a life of tranquil ease in the midst of his family and in his native town."

Offers indeed were made. In 1795 Washington's cabinet was in shambles, and men of ability thought twice before accepting national office. Marshall was no exception. He declined the posts of attorney general in 1795 and of minister to France in 1796. Washington had wanted him to replace Randolph as secretary of state in 1795 and to serve on the commission, provided for in Jay's treaty, to settle British debts. Knowing of Marshall's disinclination, the president did not make the offers. Marshall continued to advise Washington on Virginia politics and appointments, but he showed no other ambition. Virginia fully occupied his time and energy. In addition to local civic duties and attendance at the House of Delegates, he faced the considerable demands of a practice which earned him about $5,000 yearly.

In the spring of 1796 Marshall was deeply involved, personally and professionally, with the Fairfax estate. Because Baron Thomas Fairfax had been popular, Virginia considered him an American citizen and exempted his lands from its confiscation legislation. On his death in 1781 the title passed to his heir, the Reverend Denny Martin Fairfax. When the clergyman came to claim his estate, the Virginia legislature ruled that the exemption had died with Lord Fairfax and that his heir, as an English citizen, had no right to any land held prior to the Revolution.

Denny Fairfax retained Marshall as his lawyer in 1790 and began litigation to secure his title both to the manor lands, for which specific claims had been made, and to ungranted wilderness lands. The legislature had spoken of both in denying the title but seemed more interested in the wilderness lands—in 1789 Virginia had granted 788 of those acres to David Hunter. Acting on Marshall's advice to claim everything, Denny Fairfax challenged the Hunter grant on the grounds that the peace treaty of 1783 had restored all British possessions to their owners. The state courts upheld the Fairfax title, and in 1796 Hunter appealed to the Supreme Court of the United States. In the interim Marshall had joined the syndicate that had agreed to purchase the Fairfax lands—some 160,000 acres for approximately $20,000. When Hunter postponed his appeal, James Marshall went to Europe to negotiate a loan to conclude the transaction, and John worked out an arrangement to secure the title in Virginia. In December 1796 he and the legislature compromised; the Fairfax purchasers surrendered claims to the ungranted lands, and the state granted clear title to the manor lands. James finally managed a loan in April 1797 that permitted partial payment and the first steps toward completion of the transaction. Shortly thereafter, when their partner Robert Morris declared bankruptcy, the entire burden fell upon the shoulders of the Marshall brothers.

In June 1797, after nearly a decade of declining offers of national office, Marshall accepted appointment as envoy to France. For his services as minister to France he ultimately received nearly $20,000, roughly the amount owed Denny Fairfax. Marshall accepted the post because "he felt a very deep interest in the state of the controversy with France." He also confessed "that the *éclat* which would attend a successful termination of the differences between the two countries" had no small influence upon him. In addition, like a good eighteenth-century man of affairs, he planned to mix public and private business. He hoped to stop in London on the return trip; and the mission would be of such short duration that it would not interfere with his practice—that is, with his efforts to make the necessary money to keep the Fairfax venture alive.

He proved wrong on almost every count. The mission did not relieve the tension with France, it took nearly a year to fail, and it did not permit a stopover at London. But it resulted in tremendous acclaim, and the effects totally changed John Marshall's life.

IV

National Hero

1797–1801

THE XYZ AFFAIR marked the turning point in Marshall's public life. He returned from France in June 1798 a national hero and moved from Congress to the cabinet. Finally, in January 1801, he assumed the chief justiceship of the Supreme Court. The carefully planned law career was put aside. In an atmosphere of mounting domestic and international tension, Marshall had reluctantly sacrificed personal ambition to patriotic duty. "Oh God," he wrote Polly, "how much time and how much happiness have I thrown away?"

* * *

The alarming deterioration in Franco-American relations set off a diplomatic and political crisis that dominated the administration of John Adams. Angered by Jay's treaty, the French began to pillage American shipping and once more clumsily intervened in the domestic politics of the United States. In the fall of 1796 the French minister, Pierre Adet, publicly urged the election of Jefferson. Announcing the suspension of diplomatic relations to the press, he boldly hinted that a change of party would ease the tension between the two republics. Like the Genêt affair three years before, this contretemps precipitated a furious partisan exchange.

Washington, meantime, had outraged both the French and Republicans by recalling the Francophile James Monroe as minister to France. Washington then sent Charles Cotesworth Pinckney off with detailed instructions to protest both French pillage and interference in American politics. In December 1796 the French refused to receive the new minister and expelled him from the country. News of these events reached Philadelphia within a week after Adams's inauguration.

On May 16 Adams reported these indignities to a special session of Congress. The speech, according to Marshall, was "well adapted to the occasion." Referring particularly to the French disposition to separate the people from their government, Adams carefully and sternly promised the Congress that he would tolerate no further indignities. "Such attempts," he said, "ought to be repelled with a decision which shall convince France and the world that we are not a degraded people, humiliated under a colonial spirit of fear and sense of inferiority, fitted to be the miserable instruments of foreign influence, and regardless of national honor, character, and interest." He would seek peace but not at the expense of national honor. One more mission to France would attempt to heal the rupture, but if that failed, he told Congress, he wanted legislation to prepare for war.

Adams had the political good sense to recognize that no single minister would satisfy all parties. The delegation therefore reflected partisan and sectional divisions within the United States. Pinckney, a Federalist from South Carolina, continued the mission and served as its head; John Marshall represented the middle states; and Elbridge Gerry, Adams's old friend and a Massachusetts Republican, provided both balance and support.

Marshall did not receive the news of his appointment enthusiastically. For the first time in his life he did not immediately decline an appointment to national office. In the end, he joined the mission because of his concern about the mounting domestic agitation over the French question. Partisan recriminations had become so heated that, according to Jefferson, "men who have been intimate all their lives cross the streets to avoid meeting, and turn their heads another way, lest they should be obliged to touch their hats." Hope of repairing a divided nation brought Marshall to the new delegation.

One incident that spring epitomized the danger. Back in April 1796 Jefferson had written to an Italian friend, Philip Mazzei, praising France as America's "true mother country" and criticizing the pro-British, "monarchical" tendencies of the Washington administration. The government, he said, was largely in the hands of "men who were Samsons in the field and Solomons in the council, but who have had their heads shorn by the harlot England." Mazzei gave the letter to the press, and it appeared in the Paris *Moniteur* early in 1797. The *Moniteur* accepted the letter as an explanation of American foreign policy and a justification of French retaliation. When the Federalist press reprinted the letter in May, Jefferson became the center of a partisan storm. Shocked at the letter's virulence, Marshall never forgave Jefferson for charging Washington with defection from the principles of the American Revolution. More worrisome, Jefferson's letter had convinced the French that a deep division existed between the government and the people of the United States. Marshall feared that this belief would encourage France to greater exertions to force the United States from neutrality. He spent the next year trying to persuade the French of American determination for independence.

On the way to receive Adams's instructions, Marshall had paused at Mount Vernon to confer with Washington, who wrote him a letter of introduction to Pinckney. Marshall, Washington wrote, was "a firm friend, upon true principles to his country, sensible and discreet." Upon arriving at the capital, Marshall dined privately with President Adams. At this first meeting, the two men received favorable impressions of one another. Next evening Marshall dined with his Fairfax partner, Robert Morris, and then celebrated the Fourth of July at a dinner with congressional leaders. Almost a month had passed since over fifty of his friends had sent him off from Richmond with a gala dinner at the Eagle Tavern, and still the sailing arrangements had not been completed. He spent his time attending the theater and longing for the comforts left behind in Richmond. "My dearest Polly," he wrote, "I am beyond expression impatient to set out on the embassy. . . . This dissipated life does not long suit my temper. . . . I wish to Heaven . . . we were looking back on our separation instead of seeing it before us." Finally, on July 18, he set sail—determined to use his "utmost endeavors" to bring peace by Christmas.

While he crossed, a constitutional crisis was building in France. A five-man executive body, the Directory, had come to power in 1795 in a reaction to the Reign of Terror. In the first real test of their government in March 1797, a sizable opposition had returned a legislature committed to peace and to a reconciliation with the United States. In the ensuing months the Directory and the legislature drew apart on foreign policy matters. On September 4, the day after Marshall joined Pinckney at The Hague, the Directory broke, voided the March elections, purged two of its members, and restricted criticism of the government. The coup placed the government in the hands of three Directors—all hostile to the United States.

Such was the ominous beginning of Marshall's mission. Despite their forebodings, Marshall and Pinckney proceeded to Paris, where Gerry finally joined them on October 4. Four days later the trio met for the first time with the Directory's new foreign minister, Charles Maurice de Talleyrand-Périgord—avaricious, cunning, and venal, the consummate diplomat. Talleyrand politely informed the Americans that he preferred to postpone negotiations for several days until the Directory approved his recommendations on American affairs. A week later, Marshall noted that "our reception is postponed in a manner most unusual & contemptuous."

The three Americans never were accorded an official

reception. Days, then weeks passed; still Talleyrand refused to see them. Instead, he "assailed" the delegation with his agents—immortalized in the published dispatches as "X," "Y," and "Z." These intermediaries informed the American ministers that Adams's May speech had irritated the Directors. Formal negotiations, they said, could not begin until the Americans repudiated the obnoxious parts of the speech and agreed to a $12 million loan and a $250,000 bribe to Talleyrand and the Directors. "History," Marshall wrote later, "will scarcely furnish an example of a nation, not absolutely degraded, which has received from a foreign power such open contumely, and undisguised insult, as were, on this occasion, suffered by the United States in the persons of their ministers."

For months Talleyrand toyed with the Americans. It was necessary, he felt, to impress the United States with the full extent of French anger at Jay's treaty. Other events strengthened his hand. In late October, Napoleon, then twenty-eight and just beginning his remarkable career, forced a humiliating treaty on Austria and confirmed French military mastery of Europe. When that news reached Paris, Talleyrand's agents increased their pressure, adding intimidation to the "open contumely, and undisguised insult" Marshall had noted earlier. Blustering about an invasion of England, they threatened war, hinted at personal violence to the ministers, and warned about the strength of the French party in the United States. Marshall wrote despondently to Washington that "only the Atlantic can save us."

Each day spent with X, Y, and Z postponed negotiation and allowed the continued French plunder of American ships. The American ministers had come to engage in formal negotiations to preserve American neutrality, and Marshall argued that they did not have the authority to agree to unofficial prerequisites compromising the absolute sovereignty of the United States "in matters of policy, commerce, and government." Yet such compromise was the French intent. Marshall refused to be coerced into surrender. "My own private opinion," he wrote Secretary of State Timothy Pickering, "is that this haughty ambitious government . . . will not condescend to act with justice or to treat us as a free & independent nation."

Marshall and Pinckney, determined not to yield to French pressure, went along with Gerry's ultraconciliatory personal diplomacy. Forbearance, Marshall explained to United States Minister to Great Britain Rufus King, might produce some good, and it would clearly demonstrate that the Americans had made every effort to reach an accommodation compatible with honor. But he also warned that "submission has its limits, and if we have not actually passed we are certainly approaching them."

A long memorial to Talleyrand made a "last effort" to lay the American case before the French government. Dispassionately, and with powerful logic, Marshall defended neutrality during the wars of the French Revolution. He emphasized the grievances against France, beginning with Genêt's impudent meddling and continuing through the sordid treatment of the ministers, who still sought accommodation. If that were impossible, they would go home. The statement went to Talleyrand on January 31, 1798.

Marshall did not expect to impress Talleyrand. With failure of the mission imminent and the French question an explosive issue in the United States, he believed it essential to present the controversy fairly and fully to the American public. He wanted to demonstrate that the Adams administration had earnestly sought peace and that France had held the United States in contempt. He agreed with Washington that "the mass of our citizens require no more than to understand a question to decide it properly; and an adverse conclusion of the negotiation will have this effect."

Talleyrand delayed a formal reply and personally pressed the loan demand in a series of flattering private discussions with Gerry, whom he planned to use to divide the mission and to force Marshall and Pinckney out of France. He succeeded.

After nearly six months of marking time, Marshall was impatient. When the New Englander suggested in February that they agree to the loan, he exploded. "I told him," recorded Marshall in his journal, "that my judgment was not more convinced that the floor was wood, or that I stood on my feet and not on my head, than that our instructions would not permit us to make the loan required." At Marshall's insistence the ministers finally met with Talleyrand during the first week in March. Now the foreign minister directly told them the loan was indispensable. The Americans repeated what they had said in the memorial nearly six weeks before. They would not agree.

At length, on March 20, Talleyrand answered the American memorial with an irritating and insulting letter designed, like Marshall's, for American consumption. In the current crisis, Talleyrand argued, the government of the United States had sought to prevent a restoration of friendly relations by appointing to its delegation members of the English political faction. He proposed, Marshall noted wryly, "that two of us should go home leaving for the negotiation the person most acceptable to France."

The Americans agreed that Marshall should draft a strong reply denying Talleyrand's charges—especially of their partiality to Great Britain—and asserting for the last time that none of the commissioners had authority to negotiate alone. But Talleyrand's emissaries continued to threaten war unless Gerry stayed. Unmoved, Marshall and Pinckney made plans to leave Paris as soon as they could force the foreign minister to send their passports. Gerry vacillated and in the end decided to stay in a private capacity to prevent war. His decision provoked several heated exchanges. When Pinckney accused Gerry of embarrassing the United States, Gerry retorted that his colleagues had not been honest with him. All three signed Marshall's reply, however, and sent it to Talleyrand on April 3.

Marshall spent several more weeks sparring with Talleyrand for his passport. Pinckney, whose daughter was ailing, requested permission to remain in the south of France until she regained her health. Gerry, confident of receiving new instructions from Adams, remained in Paris until July. Finally, Marshall left for Bordeaux, "happy to bid an eternal adieu to Europe." On April 24 he sailed for home on the *Alexander Hamilton,* which, he told Pinckney, was "a very excellent vessel but for the sin of name."

Paris had held a certain fascination for the affable, forty-two-year-old Virginian. Always eager to tip a glass and to engage in lighthearted conversation and repartee, Marshall had found abundant opportunity in that "gay metropolis." Although unable to speak French, he had made friends easily—even with Talleyrand's intriguers, once they moved beyond talk of bribes and loans. In late November he and Gerry had taken rooms with Madame Villette, an attractive, thirty-five-year-old widow who was Voltaire's adopted daughter—some said more—and a Talleyrand agent. This "very amiable" lady sat with the Americans several hours each afternoon and rendered, Marshall said, "'my situation less unpleasant." The Paris salons, sights, and theaters afforded a respite from the tedium of diplomatic intrigue and presented "an incessant round of amusement & dissipation." "Every day," Marshall wrote Polly, "you may see something new, magnificent and beautiful, every night you may see a spectacle which astonishes and enchants the imagination. The most lively fancy aided by the strongest description cannot equal the reality of the opera."

Still he had been lonely. Paris could not ease the pain of separation from Polly, his children, and his friends. Marshall worried particularly about the effect of his absence on his wife's precarious emotional health. In July, shortly before he had sailed for France, she had written that she suspected she was pregnant with their seventh child, and pregnancies were always difficult for Polly. After that letter, no further word had come. Marshall's ignorance of events did not lessen his anxiety. In fact, in February 1798, while Polly was recovering from the birth of a son named John Marshall, her father, Jaquelin Ambler, had died. Without the support of her husband, she had become deeply melancholy. To brighten her spirits, the family had taken her to the Frederick County home of Marshall's sister, Elizabeth Colston, in late spring.

Word had been slow in coming from Marshall in France as well. Anxiety and pessimism about the French mission had mounted steadily in the United States. Marshall's dispatches did not reach Adams until March 4, 1798. The long silence from Paris, together with rumors of failure and scattered intelligence about European affairs, inflamed party bitterness. The Congress was divided and embittered. Yet it was impossible to act without word from France. The tense situation exploded when the dispatches finally arrived. Adams informed Congress that the negotiations had failed in spite of diligent American efforts and announced a state of limited hostilities against France. Republicans mounted a determined effort in the House of Representatives to block the president's policy. On both sides pressure grew for Adams to submit the full text of the dispatches to Congress. Republicans believed he had held back information; extreme Federalists, known as "High Federalists," wanted to use the dispatches to discredit France and their political opponents. Responding to a congressional resolution, Adams revealed the whole sordid record of bribery, insult, and intrigue. The effect, Marshall noted laconically, was "warm and extensive." Republicans were astonished at the record of French diplomacy. Fisher Ames commented gleefully that the dispatches confounded the Republicans, and "the trimmers dropt off from the party, like windfalls from an apple tree in September."

An anti-French tide swept the country. Public meetings everywhere denounced French treachery, and a flood of petitions for war engulfed Adams and the Congress, which pushed through a series of defense measures including the creation of a provisional army and the establishment of a navy department. The country appeared eager for war.

Marshall was unaware of this frenzied activity when the *Alexander Hamilton* slipped into New York harbor on June 17, 1798. He immediately set out for Philadelphia to give Adams a personal report on the mission. But word of his arrival preceded him. The next day, while still some miles outside the capital, he was met by the secretary of state, three corps of cavalry in full dress, and "a concourse of citizens in carriages, on horseback, and on foot." When this caravan reached the capital, church bells pealed, cannon thundered, and exultant throngs escorted Marshall through the streets. President Adams sent a special message to Congress expressing his pleasure over Marshall's safe arrival, and a stream of admiring senators, congressmen, and distinguished citizens congratulated him at his hotel.

He was a national hero. Federalists in Congress staged a testimonial dinner in his honor at O'Eller's Tavern, and over 120 enthusiasts—including the cabinet, the justices of the Supreme Court, officers of the army, and two bishops of the American Episcopal Church—attended. The thirteenth toast of the evening became immortalized in American history: "Millions for Defense but not a cent for Tribute." After Marshall retired for the night, the assembly drank a final tribute to "The Man whom his country delights to honor."

Vice President Jefferson was conspicuously absent. The Republican leader could not bring himself to celebrate a Federalist triumph. Even so, he twice called unsuccessfully at Marshall's hotel that morning to pay his respects in person.

The war fever worried Marshall, who still believed peace the most pressing need of the United States. Marshall informed Adams and Pickering of his conviction that the Directory would not declare war and would continue to force American compliance through intimidation. He cautioned against precipitate action. Once the Directory saw that the United States could not be intimidated and that the people stood firmly behind the president, he told Adams, France might be more conciliatory. The assessment proved accurate. By the fall of 1798 Talleyrand had indicated a willingness to receive another American mission. More important, Marshall's advice had dissuaded the president from seeking a declaration of war and had also persuaded extreme Federalists to abandon their clamor.

News of Polly's collapse clouded the celebration. The endless parade of well-wishers and the countless accolades and addresses only delayed his return to her side and to his newborn son and their other children. Impatient to be gone, Marshall paid a quick visit to his old friend and partner Robert Morris, now in debtors' prison, and set out for Virginia and his long-awaited reunion with Polly.

Jubilant crowds cheered his arrival at every stop on the homeward journey. The Richmond reception rivaled that at Philadelphia. Miles outside the city he was met by military units, the governor and council, and throngs of ordinary folk eager to catch a glimpse of Richmond's most famous citizen. A public meeting was held in his honor, and Marshall made an impressive speech castigating French duplicity and urging Americans to support their government.

"I returned to Richmond," Marshall recalled, "with a full determination to devote myself entirely to my professional duties, and was not a little delighted to find that my prospects at the bar had sustained no material injury from my absence." Almost as soon as he returned home, however, Virginia again boiled with controversy over the Alien and Sedition Acts of July 1798. The Federalist majority in Congress exploited the political windfall of the XYZ affair by enlarging the army and navy, suspending trade with France, setting aside all treaties with the former ally, and enacting a direct tax on property to pay for these measures. Intense partisanship generated an intolerance both repressive and impolitic. "It is Patriotism to write in favor of our government," proclaimed the leading Federalist journal, "it is sedition to write against it." The Alien and Sedition Acts incorporated this attitude into the law. The Alien Act authorized the president to deport dangerous aliens. The more controversial Sedition Act imposed heavy fines and imprisonment on anyone convicted in federal court for writing, printing, publishing, or even uttering "any false, scandalous, and malicious" statements defaming a member or branch of the government of the United States.

John Marshall perceived that the Sedition Act was a blunder more likely to consolidate than stifle opposition. A long letter to Secretary of State Pickering in August reported that Virginia Republicans were attacking the constitutionality of the act and gaining ground. Even "many well intentioned men" believed the law "unwarranted by the Constitution." By September Federalists were losing the support they had enjoyed just two months before. Richmond Federalists pressed Marshall to run for Congress in 1799, well aware that even one more vote in the House might prove crucial. He declined. "My refusal was peremptory," he said, "and I did not believe it possible that my determination could be shaken. I was however mistaken."

George Washington intervened. The aging hero believed the scurrilous Republican opposition fully justified the repressive legislation, and he exerted his influence to get good Federalists elected to the state and national legislatures. He invited his nephew Bushrod Washington and Marshall to Mount Vernon on September 3. For three days he pressed their candidacy. His nephew assented, but Marshall resisted "on the ground of my situation, & the necessity of attending to my pecuniary affairs." The former president, Marshall recalled later, stressed that national crises "made it the duty of the citizen to forego his private for the public interest." Washington himself had come out of retirement to command the new provisional army. Finally, unable to resist Washington's persistent urgings, Marshall yielded and began his campaign for Congress.

Two weeks later President Adams offered Marshall the seat on the Supreme Court vacated by the death of Associate Justice James Wilson. Marshall, unwilling to accept the $3,500 salary of an associate justice, declined. Bushrod Washington filled the vacancy.

Marshall's race against the Republican incumbent, John

Clopton, differed markedly from his earlier forays into politics. In those contests for the state legislature as a representative of Richmond, his local popularity and prominence were tremendous assets. An election for national office involved a wider area, including overwhelmingly Republican districts outside Richmond—a decisive handicap in such a partisan campaign. Inevitably, Marshall became the target for vicious abuse. He was the most famous Federalist in the South, perhaps in the nation, and Republicans spared no effort to defeat him. He was stung by the acid manner of the attack and appalled at assertions that the government of the United States was a more formidable enemy to liberty than the French Directory. He complained of the Republican press teeming with poisonous attacks.

But Marshall also used the press in his campaign. In September 1798 Virginia newspapers carried a letter by "A Freeholder" asking whether Marshall had been an advocate of the Alien and Sedition bills and whether he would use his influence to obtain a repeal in the event of his election. Marshall himself had written the letter to get his position before his constituents. His carefully worded answers a week later showed his political acumen, good sense, and uncompromising independence. "I am not," he declared, "an advocate for the Alien and Sedition bills." Had he been in Congress when they were passed, he continued, he would have opposed them—not because they were "fraught with all those mischiefs which many gentlemen ascribe to them," but because they were useless and "calculated only to create unnecessary discontents and jealousies at a time when our very existence as a nation, may depend on our union." He did not advocate repeal, because the acts would automatically expire in March 1801. But he would "obey the voice of my constituents" and "indisputably oppose their revival."

The answer to "A Freeholder" circulated widely, but, clever as it was, it satisfied no one. Republicans pointed out that Marshall had skirted their main objection—the unconstitutionality of the laws. Federalist bigwigs, demanding strict adherence to party, called the exchange of letters a cheap electioneering trick. John Marshall had defied his party and was the only Federalist in 1798 to express any reservations about the Alien and Sedition laws. "No correct man,—no incorrect man, even—whose affections are wedded to the government, would give his name to the base opposers of the law," the eloquent Fisher Ames commented angrily.

The campaign grew more heated during the winter session of the Virginia legislature. Protest meetings that summer had petitioned the legislature to protest the constitutionality of the laws. But Republican leaders were convinced that some stronger effort was necessary.

Collaborating secretly, Jefferson and Madison made the Kentucky and Virginia resolutions formal legislative protests against the "unconstitutional and obnoxious" acts. The resolutions summarized the Republican principles of state sovereignty and strict interpretation. The national government possessed only delegated powers. All other powers—including authority to remove aliens and control of the press—were reserved to the states, which had a right to judge congressional usurpations of power and to seek redress. The resolutions asked other states to join in a concerted protest.

The talk about states' rights alarmed the Federalists. Marshall, for one, believed the Republicans had finally shown their true colors. In January he wrote Washington that Republicans preferred disunion to "a continuance of an administration not of their own party." Federalist criticism impressed Republicans with the need for a fuller statement of the grounds for their opposition. Madison's *Address of the General Assembly to the People,* distributed at government expense, reviewed Federalist administrations since Washington. It demonstrated that Hamilton's fiscal policies, the Jay treaty, and now the hated Alien and Sedition Acts pointed toward consolidation, monarchy, and the subversion of popular liberties. Only a Republican administration could save the nation from tyranny. Marshall and Henry Lee countered with an *Address from the Minority,* distributed by Federalists at their own expense.

The Marshall–Lee paper argued that the national government was "indubitably limited as to its objects" but not to the means "necessary and proper" to attain those objects. Any inquiry into whether the law exceeded the powers delegated to the national government had to recognize that a Constitution meant to endure for ages contained general expressions, not minute detail. "In reviewing then our constitution, to decide on the powers vested for general purposes, we must examine it fairly, but liberally." Otherwise the government would be impotent. The common law authorized punishment for seditious libel, and even Republicans admitted state power over sedition at common law. Marshall and Lee asserted that if such power were necessary to protect the people of the states from the highly destructive effects of "malignant falsehood," then it was clearly Congress's power under the "necessary and proper" clause to protect the people of the United States against the same evil. The First Amendment, they argued, did not reserve common-law prosecution for libel to the states; it prohibited Congress from making any law "respecting a religious establishment, but not from making any law respecting the press." Congress could not pass a law "abridging" liberty of the press, but that meant freedom from "previous restraint," not "the liberty of spreading with impunity false and scandalous slanders, which may destroy the peace, and mangle the reputation, of an individual or of a community."

This reasoning on freedom of the press in 1798 was an accurate statement of the then authoritative Blackstonian notion. The view was exactly what prevailed in the states before, during, and after the controversy over the Sedition Act. The Sedition Act had advanced beyond the common law by adding the protections of jury trial and truth as a defense.

While Marshall campaigned against Republicans in Virginia, a deep rift opened within Federalist ranks. In October 1798 the French indicated a willingness to receive another American minister—this time with due respect. Adams had watched his party's popularity plummet; the French overture presented an opportunity to restore its stance. Adams displayed good political judgment and courageous statesmanship in exploiting the French gesture. In February 1799, without the advice of his cabinet, the president stunned the Federalist Congress by sending another minister to France.

Infuriated High Federalists, led by Hamilton and Pickering, attempted to block the mission, for peace would threaten Federalist success in the presidential election in 1800. Adams would not yield the basic point, but he did agree to enlarge the mission, headed by Oliver Ellsworth, to include Federalist stalwarts. Marshall welcomed the president's decision. He had to win an election in Republican Virginia, and, as his independent stand on the Sedition Act had demonstrated, he stood to gain by dissociating himself from extreme Federalist positions. Adams's peace proposal enabled Marshall to argue that the vigorous administration defense measures had forced France to make the overtures Adams had accepted.

On April 3, as the election approached, Marshall wrote his brother James that victory was "extremely uncertain. The means us'd to defeat it are despicable in the extreme and yet they succeed. Nothing I believe more debases or pollutes the human mind than faction." In March Republicans learned the unfavorable responses of the other states to the Virginia Resolution and stepped up their attacks on the administration. Election day brought no relief, as voters cast their ballots in the midst of free-flowing whiskey and free-flying fists. In the most fiercely contested election in Virginia history, Marshall was victorious by the narrow margin of 108 votes. Virginia Federalists won eight of nineteen congressional seats—an impressive victory in the Republican stronghold, and a gain of four seats over the previous session.

A number of circumstances explained Marshall's close

victory, but the surge of nationalism and his reputation as a hero were decisive. Patrick Henry expressed the situation well in a widely circulated letter denouncing the Republican legislative tactics. "Tell Marshall I love him," wrote Henry, "because he felt and acted as a republican, as an American."

Domestic politics dominated the Sixth Congress as Federalists and Republicans maneuvered for the presidential election of 1800. High Federalists who controlled the Senate were still indignant at Adams's peace overture and had only reluctantly agreed to support his candidacy in 1800. In the House of Representatives most of the new Federalists were southern moderates more inclined to follow the increasingly popular Adams than High Federalist leadership. This uncertain majority confronted a reinvigorated and disciplined Republican opposition bent on exploiting the split in Federalist ranks.

In mid-December 1799, with the first session barely two weeks old, news of Washington's death plunged the capital into mourning. Marshall broke the sad tidings to the House "in a voice that bespoke the anguish of his mind, and a countenance expressive of the deepest regret." Next day he introduced Henry Lee's resolution immortalizing Washington as "first in war, first in peace, and first in the hearts of his countrymen."

Marshall distinguished himself as a vigorous, even decisive, champion of Adams against Federalist and Republican challenges. Until May 1800, when the first session adjourned to facilitate removal of the capital to the new location at Washington, D.C., Marshall was the leading administration spokesman in the House. His ability and careful attention to detail in committee forced even High Federalists to a grudging admission of his usefulness. "He possesses great powers," wrote House Speaker Theodore Sedgwick, "and has much dexterity in the application of them. In short we can do nothing without him."

Two of the most pressing matters, judicial reform and a national bankruptcy act, were left over from the preceding

Congress. Two days after Adams's address, both houses of Congress appointed committees to report judiciary and bankruptcy bills. In each house the same prominent Federalists served simultaneously on both committees. Freshman Congressman John Marshall was one of the five members on the House committees.

Pressure for these reforms arose from the economic and political problems of the 1790s. The compromise Judiciary Act of 1789 had left nationalists dissatisfied with concurrent state court jurisdiction over some federal questions and states' rights advocates upset at Section 25, which allowed appeals from state courts to the Supreme Court of the United States. A firm believer in energetic national government, an experienced lawyer, and a land speculator with large holdings, Marshall had a deep personal and political interest in judicial reform and a uniform national bankruptcy law.

By 1799 Federalists believed that the need for such laws had become urgent. The pressure grew as a result of business failures caused by the quasi-war with France and by speculative land ventures. Most states lacking insolvency laws simply imprisoned debtors, and land speculators faced judicial tests in hostile state courts. The desire to have titles litigated in sympathetic federal courts united with the law-and-order frenzy accompanying the Sedition Act to generate strong efforts at judicial reform.

When the House committee reported a bankruptcy bill in January 1800, Marshall introduced an amendment calling for a jury trial on the facts, hoping thereby to soften southern opposition. Without the amendment the bill would have failed. The Senate acted favorably in March, and Adams signed the first national bankruptcy law before leaving office.

The judiciary reform bill proposed two major reforms: an increase in the number of federal circuit courts and an expansion of their original jurisdiction—especially in cases involving land titles. Marshall gave the measure a lengthy defense, but Republicans won a postponement to the next session with the aid of some Federalists. The uncertain majority had disappeared on this vital legislation. "The dread of unpopularity" in this election year paralyzed action and prevented "the erection of additional buttresses to the Constitution."

Marshall's greatest effort during the Sixth Congress was a defense of Adams in the Thomas Nash affair. Nash had been arrested in Charleston, South Carolina, as one of a band of British sailors who had mutinied and murdered their ship's officers. British authorities requested his extradition under Article 27 of the Jay treaty; Adams complied, and Nash was hanged. The president's surrender of the prisoner outraged Republicans, who felt it an unnecessary goodwill gesture toward monarchical England. Furthermore, after his arrest in Charleston, Nash claimed to be an American citizen—Jonathan Robbins of Danbury, Connecticut, impressed into British service. He claimed he had murdered only to escape. Republicans argued that even if Nash were not American, he was entitled to a trial in American courts. They introduced a transparently political motion to censure Adams for unconstitutionally interfering with the judiciary.

The debate began in mid-February. From the outset Marshall worried over the political motives behind the censure motion. Adams testified to the House that Connecticut could find no record that a Jonathan Robbins or even a Robbins family had ever lived in Danbury. Unsatisfied, Republicans pressed for more documents until Marshall closed all argument with a speech vindicating the president on March 7.

Jay's treaty explicitly required the surrender of British subjects for crimes committed under British jurisdiction. Nations always had jurisdiction over persons serving on their high seas fleets. The only question was whether Nash's case should have been heard by the judiciary as the Republicans argued. Marshall responded with a masterful analysis of judicial power. The Constitution did not give the courts jurisdiction in all *questions* but in all *cases*. The difference was "material and apparent." A case implied limited jurisdiction.

To be a case "a question must assume a legal form for forensic litigation and judicial decision. There must be parties to come into court, who can be reached by its process, and bound by its power; whose rights admit of ultimate decision by a tribunal to which they are bound to submit." To argue otherwise would subvert the principle of separation of powers. If judicial power extended to every question under the Constitution, it would swallow the legislature; if it were to apply to every question under the laws and treaties, it would overwhelm the executive. The courts had no power in this controversy, Marshall argued, because it was a *question* concerning execution of a treaty, and it could not be a *case* if the parties were sovereign nations.

He admitted that treaties involved questions of law. But, he argued, not every question of law must necessarily be carried into court. Treaties raised "questions of political law," and the Constitution did not confer on the judiciary "any political power whatever." These political questions are "proper to be decided . . . by the Executive, and not by the courts." The president was the "sole organ of the nation in its external affairs." He possessed the "whole Executive power," and any act requiring the force of the nation must be performed through him. His judgment on such matters, Marshall concluded, was final and not reviewable elsewhere.

The opposition collapsed. When Republicans turned to Albert Gallatin, the minority leader, to answer the argument, he replied that he thought it unanswerable. The careful, lucid constitutional analysis that later characterized Marshall's judicial opinions made acceptable an interpretation "wholly unthought of when the meaning of the article was heretofore considered."

Marshall's congressional career ended shortly before the close of the first session on May 14. In late January Marshall, faithful to his campaign pledge, had voted with Republicans to repeal the Sedition Act. The Senate refused to concur, and, as Marshall had predicted, that notorious measure died unmourned in 1801.

Offered the position of secretary of war, he requested the

president to withdraw his nomination and then learned that he had been nominated and confirmed as secretary of state. Marshall's acceptance of the post was not altogether enthusiastic. He would have preferred the bar, but his practice had suffered in his absence. "I was given up as a lawyer," he wrote, "and considered generally as entirely a political man. I lost my business altogether."

As secretary of state, Marshall remained largely outside the swirl of politics. He superintended affairs in the new capital, whose swamps and general disarray made it "an ever-present reminder to the men in power of the low esteem in which power was held." In October the Ellsworth mission returned from France with a treaty annulling the 1778 alliance in return for American abandonment of claims against France. Marshall recommended ratification. The Senate complied. Problems with Britain remained to be solved: impressment, continued confiscation of ships and cargoes, and the old nettle of debts. Finally, Marshall wrote Adams's last address to Congress in December 1800 and once more stressed the need for judicial reform.

He took no part in the election. In December he commented on Adams's loss and the necessity for the House of Representatives to break the tie between Jefferson and Aaron Burr, which did not interest him. "I consider it a choice of evils and I really am uncertain which would be the greatest." He planned to return to Richmond to resume his practice as a lawyer. "If my present wish can succeed," he wrote, "I shall never again fill any political station whatever."

He never returned to his practice. On January 19, 1801, Adams nominated him as chief justice of the United States. One week later the Senate confirmed the nomination.

Prominent

V

An Independent Judiciary

1801–1806

JOHN MARSHALL had supported the Constitution in 1788 because he believed it provided for the kind of sound representative government in which the people chose their leaders on the basis of demonstrated character, judgment, and respectability. But the mounting partisanship, the pandering to popular passions, and the growth of party organizations and newspapers jeopardized the future of the Republic, in his view. "There is a tide in the affairs of nations, of parties, and of individuals," he wrote gloomily during the savage campaign of 1800. "I fear that [tide] of real Americanism is on the ebb." As chief justice for more than a third of a century, Marshall struggled to counteract the pressures of democracy and political parties by establishing the primacy of the principles that had animated the framers of the Constitution. In so doing he established the Supreme Court as a powerful branch of the national government. Paradoxically, the partisan politics he deplored generated the conflict over the judiciary that placed Marshall on the Supreme Court and dominated his first years as chief justice.

*　　*　　*

The Federalist rout in the election of 1800 became apparent shortly after the second (lame duck) session of the Sixth Congress convened in December 1800. The Federalist party had lost not only the presidency but its congressional majority. Only the judiciary remained as a bulwark against democratic excess. Certain that the Republican victory would convulse the nation, Federalist leaders strengthened the judiciary in the waning days of their majority.

The Judiciary Act of 1801, rushed through Congress and signed by John Adams on February 13, 1801—less than a month before Thomas Jefferson's inauguration—was a commendable effort at reform. In 1789 Congress had organized the federal courts hierarchically. At the top was the Supreme Court with the chief justice and five associates; at the bottom were thirteen district courts with separate judges. In between were the three circuit courts on which Supreme Court justices sat twice yearly with the local district judge. Problems arose immediately. The physical burden of riding circuit caused Supreme Court justices to resign and made appointments to the Court difficult. Regular complaints were made about the anomaly of the justices hearing on appeal the cases they had decided on circuit. By creating sixteen separate circuit court judges and enlarging the jurisdiction of their courts, the Judiciary Act of 1801 increased the efficiency and enhanced the reputation of the federal courts. The new legislation pleased Marshall because of its "separation of the judges of the supreme from those of the circuit courts."

Blatant partisanship unfortunately obscured the real merits of the act. Its timing alone was damaging. A lame duck Federalist Congress created an opportunity to pack an enlarged federal judiciary with sixteen judges holding life tenure and a train of marshals and clerks. Moreover, the act reduced the number of Supreme Court justices from six to five at the next vacancy, with the obvious intent of depriving Jefferson of an appointment until two vacancies occurred—by which time Federalists hoped to have recaptured the presidency. As if to remove any doubts about the partisan intent, Adams filled all these positions before he left office.

Adams had begun to worry about appointments before the Judiciary Act was passed. Chief Justice Oliver Ellsworth resigned in mid-December, and Adams had to fill that vacancy before the pending legislation reduced the number to five. On December 18 he appointed former Chief Justice John Jay. The Senate approved the nomination the next day, although many shared Marshall's opinion that a Jay refusal was "most probable." Adams, too, had considered this probability and planned to elevate William Cushing, the senior justice. The resulting vacancy would go to Jared Ingersoll, United States attorney for Pennsylvania and a leader of the Philadelphia bar. Cushing, however, was sixty-eight, and poor health had regularly hampered his work on the Court, so that Adams had to contend with the likelihood of his death or early retirement. It was urgent that Adams fill the Court to six before passage of the Judiciary Act. But he could do nothing without word from Jay.

Federalists in Congress were as concerned as Adams about the vacant chief justiceship and relayed their anxiety to him. Just before the bill passed the House, Adams finally received Jay's letter refusing the appointment. No room remained to maneuver. Adams had to act quickly and appoint a chief justice who would accept.

John Marshall was with Adams that day, and the president abruptly decided to nominate him. Marshall had never heard his name mentioned for the office and had never thought of it. But he was "pleased as well as surprized, and bowed in silence." His nomination went to the Senate on January 20, the day the judiciary bill passed the House.

Twenty-five years later Adams called the Marshall appointment a "gift" to the American people, the "proudest act" of his life. In 1801, however, the "gift" was simple political expediency. Marshall solved the president's immediate political problem. He had been loyal, was available, and, as secretary of state in daily contact with the president, could accept or decline without delay.

The Senate was astounded. Federalists regarded the nomination as another "wild freak" of the president they had come to distrust. They were less than impressed with the John Marshall who had asserted his independence of party by questioning the Sedition Act, by supporting peace with France, and by pursuing a moderate course during the Sixth Congress's first session. They delayed confirmation for a week in hope of pressuring Adams to change his mind but on January 27 relented and confirmed Marshall, "lest another not so qualified, and more disgusting to the Bench, should be substituted, and because it appeared that this gentleman was not privy to his own nomination."

The scant notice in the press revealed the low esteem in which people held the Supreme Court in 1801. Plagued by constant turnover and absence, the full Court was rarely present. The justices' practice of delivering seriatim, individual opinions robbed the full Court of authority. It had not established itself as the arbiter of constitutional questions.

In a letter accompanying Marshall's commission Adams requested the new chief justice to stay on as secretary of state until a successor could be appointed. Marshall agreed and, as no successor was appointed, served without pay in that capacity for the remainder of Adams's term. On February 4, 1801, two days after the opening of the Supreme Court's term, he took the seat he would occupy for the next thirty-four years. No decisions were handed down that term, and for the next month Secretary of State Marshall was busy assisting Adams in the last-minute rush to make appointments.

On February 27, with only four days of Federalist control remaining, "An Act concerning the District of Columbia" became law. It established a three-judge circuit court for the new capital and created the opportunity to appoint an unlimited number of attorneys, clerks, justices of the peace, and marshals. All together—counting judicial, military, naval, commercial, and diplomatic positions—Adams appointed 217 officeholders between December 18 and March 4. Ninety-three were to judicial and legal positions, and fifty-three of those were to the District of Columbia. On March 3, right up to its final adjournment, the Federalist Senate was still confirming Adams's appointments.

Marshall played a large part in these eleventh-hour maneuvers. As secretary of state he had the task of sealing and delivering the commissions, and he was still doing so at nine o'clock on the evening of March 3. His failure to complete the work was the immediate occasion for *Marbury* v. *Madison*. Moreover, as the president's intermediary, he had to advise on appointments, discourage current officeholders from resigning, and make certain that those appointed would accept.

Republicans were furious. They could not dissociate the unseemly haste in making appointments from the efforts of the Federalists in the House of Representatives to prevent Jefferson's election by throwing their votes to Burr. Marshall came in for criticism on both counts. Until the Burr–Jefferson tie was broken on February 17—after thirty-six consecutive ballots in six days—false rumors had placed Marshall in a cabal which sought to deadlock the House and then have the Congress appoint some Federalist as president. There was more truth in the charge of nepotism. Marshall's brother James was appointed a circuit judge for the District of Columbia together with William Cranch, Adams's nephew by marriage. Two Marshall brothers-in-law also became circuit judges. Even so, those appointed were generally men of ability whose politics were as moderate as those of their patrons.

"Today the new political year commences—The new order of things begins," Marshall wrote on the morning of March 4, 1801. He was about to administer the oath of office to Thomas Jefferson, and he was anxious for the future of the Republic. "The democrats," he continued, "are divided into speculative theorists & absolute terrorists. With the latter I am not disposed to class Mr. Jefferson. If he arranges himself with them it is not difficult to foresee that much calamity is in store for our country—if he does not they will soon become his enemies and calumniators."

Federalists—and Republicans—in 1801 were uncertain about the peaceful transfer of power. Convinced of the fragility of responsible government, Federalists believed that the Jeffersonian "artificers of ruin" planned the systematic destruction of commerce, capital, the military, and the judiciary.

Many Republicans did interpret their victory in 1800 as a mandate for radical reform. Only substantial change could reverse Federalist perversion of the principles of the Revolution. More moderate Republicans, Jefferson and Madison among them, were content to trust in the change of men in government. All Republicans had serious complaints about the Federalist judiciary, but they differed on means of redress. Moderates protested the behavior of partisan judges but did not wish to jeopardize the independence of the judiciary. Deaths and resignations would, in time, bring fair-minded judges to the federal bench. Radicals like William Branch Giles of Virginia argued that nothing short of "an absolute repeal of the whole Judiciary and terminating the present offices and creating a new system" would "redress the evil system." Giles was particularly critical of the "misapplied idea" of judicial independence.

These radical proposals suggested absolute terrorism to Marshall. If this implacable hostility to the judicial and legal systems became a part of the "new order," nothing would be left to check popular passions. Anarchy was just over the horizon.

The posture of the new president was crucial, and Marshall listened with some apprehension to the inaugural address. "Every difference of opinion is not a difference of principle," Jefferson said. "We have called by different names brethren of the same principle. We are all republicans: we are all federalists." The tone of the address, its disparagement of party, clearly placed the new executive among the moderates. Relieved, Marshall thought it "well judged and conciliatory, . . . giving the lie to the violent party declamation which has elected him, but . . . strongly characteristic of the general cast of his political theory."

These two Virginians actually had a great deal in common—beyond a mutual dislike that intensified with the years and the characteristic Virginia carelessness in attire. Both had absorbed the doctrines of liberal individualism set forth by Locke, Montesquieu, and Hume. They believed that society existed to protect the individual's natural rights. They stressed limited government, including separation of powers and an independent judiciary to protect the individual against majority excesses. Both, too, sought to preserve the federal Union, although Marshall worried more about the centrifugal tendencies in the states and Jefferson about the corruption and centralization in the national government.

Their philosophical differences arose from contrary views of human nature. "Those who know human nature, black as it is," Marshall said in his speech on the judiciary at the Virginia Convention in 1788, "must know that mankind . . . are attached to their own interests"—life, liberty of movement and opinion, and the opportunity to acquire property. An ordered and progressive society had to ignore fleeting passions and speculative theories and coldly organize itself to protect these mundane interests. Marshall had no faith in a "victory of reason over passion." He agreed wholeheartedly with Madison's statement in the tenth *Federalist* essay that the "first object of government" was "the protection of different and unequal faculties of acquiring property." Marshall wanted leadership by a natural aristocracy that earned power, wealth, and status in the competitive free market.

Jefferson was more optimistic and humanitarian, more flexible and egalitarian. He preferred the "pursuit of happiness" to the protection of property and was more willing than Marshall to limit the acquisitions of the few to ease the suffering of the many.

Jefferson was as prone as the Federalists to exaggerate his opponents' danger to the Republic. Vexed and disappointed that his old friend Adams had made so many "midnight" appointments, Jefferson determined that this "outrage on decency should not have its effect, except in life appointments [judges] which are irremovable." He immediately replaced the Federalist marshals and attorneys with Republicans. He also reduced Adams's forty-two justices of the peace to thirty but retained twenty-five of the original appointees. One of those eliminated was William Marbury, whose commission Marshall had carelessly failed to deliver. Toward the judges Jefferson remained moderate. His actions through 1801 indicated that he had not yet determined to endorse radical desires to repeal the Judiciary Act of 1801.

Two weeks after the inauguration Marshall expressed "infinite chagrin" over Jefferson's decision to withhold the undelivered commissions. He admitted Jefferson's authority to cancel the appointments of attorneys and marshals. The term of the justices of the peace had been fixed by statute at five years, and Marshall believed this law removed the president's discretion in their cases. His disappointment sprang from embarrassment that "some blame may be imputed to me."

At the first session of the new circuit court for the District of Columbia in June 1801, the two Federalist judges took an extraordinary step. James Marshall and William Cranch ordered the district attorney to begin a libel prosecution against the editor of the *National Intelligencer,* the newly established administration newspaper, for slander against the judiciary. Since the Sedition Act had expired, they ordered the indictment at common law. William Kilty, the third judge and a Jeffersonian, refused to go along. The Republican district attorney refused to prosecute; the grand jury refused to indict; and the matter was dropped in September. But Republicans saw once again a partisan bench using the hated common law to squelch political opposition.

Before passions cooled, the new circuit court in Connecticut upheld its clerk's refusal to execute a Jefferson order in a prize case. Federalist newspapers crowed over this judicial halt to executive usurpation. Jefferson smoldered at another political jab by midnight judges. Unwittingly, the Federalists removed the doubts of many moderate Republicans about the wisdom of repealing the Judiciary Act of 1801.

The unremitting partisan discussion forced Jefferson to address the problem in his first message to Congress. As yet, however, he was still reluctant to suggest changes which might endanger judicial independence. He surprised Federalists and radical Republicans by merely hinting that Congress should pay some attention to the judiciary, especially the portion "recently erected."

At this critical juncture, with Jefferson and moderate congressional Republicans still hesitant, the Federalists blundered in the case of *Marbury* v. *Madison*. Marbury and three other justices of the peace whose commissions Jefferson had refused to deliver brought suit in the Supreme Court seeking a writ of mandamus (an order) requiring Secretary of State Madison to deliver their commissions. On December 17 their attorney presented a preliminary motion for a court ruling requiring Madison to show cause why the writ should not issue against him. After considering the matter for one day, the chief justice gave the Court's opinion, issued the usual order, and assigned the fourth day of the next term for argument on the question of whether Marbury was entitled to the writ.

In ordinary circumstances such a routine petition and order might have passed quietly into obscurity. But December 1801 was not an ordinary time. The timing of the suit and the mounting Federalist anxiety over a probable repeal of the 1801 act suggest that Marbury's suit was part of an effort to intimidate the president by challenging the constitutionality of his refusal to deliver the commissions.

Marshall's first *Marbury* decision excited widespread indignation and was the immediate cause for the repeal of the 1801 Judiciary Act. Even moderate Republicans thought it a "bold stroke" against the executive and a "high-handed exertion of Judiciary power." This preliminary ruling also convinced Jefferson that the pretensions of the judiciary must be curbed. The Federalists had "retired into the Judiciary as a stronghold . . . and from that battery all the works of Republicanism are to be beaten down and erased." The new Congress swiftly moved to repeal.

On January 6, 1802, Senator John Breckinridge of Kentucky introduced a motion to repeal the Judiciary Act of 1801. For almost two months that question monopolized the attention of Congress. The debates were long, impassioned, occasionally eloquent, and loaded with partisan recriminations, but they also provided a searching discussion of the relation of the courts to the other branches of government. Passage of the Repeal bill on March 3 ended the congressional debate. It did not resolve the controversy.

The fundamental question was whether Congress held the power to deprive judges of their offices by abolishing the circuit courts. Federalists argued that the Repeal Act was unconstitutional, because the Constitution guaranteed all federal judges tenure during good behavior. By abolishing the office, the judge would be removed unconstitutionally. Republicans, worried about judicial obstructionism, countered that the Constitution granted Congress discretionary power to establish and abolish inferior courts. Federalists argued further that an independent judiciary was the keystone of the constitutional system. By limiting security of tenure, Republicans opened the door to legislative oppression. The Federalists therefore threatened that the Supreme Court would be bound to declare the Repeal Act unconstitutional. Republicans had earlier deplored the unwillingness of federal courts to rule against the constitutionality of the Sedition Act. Now they responded that judicial review would lead to despotism.

The true check on congressional excesses was in the state legislatures and in the people, and they warned of impeachments if the Court dared to declare the Repeal Act unconstitutional.

Federalist threats of Supreme Court action alarmed Republicans. The 1801 act had changed the Supreme Court terms from February and August to December and June. Because the Repeal Act was not to take effect until July, the coming June term would provide an opportunity for a judicial strike. An Amendatory Act in April met that threat by eliminating the June term and establishing one annual term in February. The Court would not meet again until February 1803. The Amendatory Act also increased the number of circuit courts to six. Beyond those changes, the repeal of the 1801 act had simply restored the 1789 act.

Chief Justice Marshall presided over five other Federalists on the Supreme Court. William Cushing of Massachusetts was the last of the original six justices appointed by Washington and the last American to wear the full English judicial wig. William Paterson, a former governor of New Jersey, came to the Court in 1793. Samuel Chase was the most imposing and the most controversial member of the Court. Called "Bacon Face" because of his ruddy complexion, the massive, white-haired Marylander was high-handed, inflammatory, and irascible. His advocacy of the Sedition Act and his harangues to grand juries in sedition trials on circuit made him the symbol of blatant judicial partisanship to Republicans. Marshall's close friend and fellow Virginian Bushrod Washington had come to the Court in 1798. Small in stature and deferential to the chief justice during the thirty-one years he spent on the Bench, Washington was an able judge. Last and least was Alfred Moore. This distinguished North Carolinian was appointed in 1799 and resigned in 1801, leaving practically no trace.

Marshall was less upset than many Federalists by the Repeal Act. "There are some essential defects in the [1789] system which I presume will be remedied," he wrote on April 5, "as they involve no part of political questions but relate only the mode of carrying causes from the circuit to the supreme court." Those problems had concerned him since before the passage of the 1801 act. Now he had "no doubt" the moderate Republicans would remedy them again. The Amendatory Act did not live up to his expectations. He would have to ride the fifth circuit and hold court at Richmond in May and November and at Raleigh, North Carolina, in June and December.

By dispossessing the circuit judges the Repeal Act had raised a serious constitutional question. But Marshall believed that the law must be tolerated and that the 1801 circuit courts should close their doors at the end of their spring sessions. This stance was a frank recognition of political realities. Any partisan move by the Court, real or apparent, would only antagonize the more powerful Republicans. His circumspection was the product of temperament and of a canvass of the other justices' views. Marshall had persuaded his colleagues to abandon seriatim opinions. He wanted the justices to confer on each case, reach a consensus, and speak authoritatively through a single majority opinion rather than express their individual opinions. This impression of impeccable unity would enhance the Court's authority.

Marshall had constitutional scruples about performing circuit court duties and was personally inclined not to resume them, but he was unwilling to refuse "without a consultation of the Judges." Exchanges with Paterson, Cushing, and Washington convinced the chief justice that the majority believed policy dictated acquiescence. Chase alone urged resistance, but in the end that old Federalist diehard deferred to the majority.

The Federalist justices also refused to accede to partisan plans to frustrate the Republicans by a declaration that the commissions of the 1801 circuit judges had been unconstitutionally vacated. In September, Bushrod Washington, on circuit in Hartford, Connecticut, refused the gambit. Cushing followed suit some time later at Boston. On December 2, 1802, Marshall did the same in *Stuart* v. *Laird* at Richmond. He dismissed the argument against congressional power to require circuit court duties of Supreme Court justices, and the case went to the Supreme Court on a writ of error.

High Federalists were chagrined. George Cabot wrote that the justices' display of independence demonstrated that not even "good men" could be counted on "to support our system of policy and government." The Republican press had a field day celebrating the decisions.

But Marshall had acquitted himself well. The Court not only had acted in harmony but also had preserved its independence in the face of intense partisan pressure. He completed his trip on circuit and encountered less weighty problems. Arriving at "Rawleigh," he wrote Polly of his mortification at discovering that he had lost fifteen silver dollars from his waistcoat pocket. "They had worn through the various mendings the pocket had sustained & sought their liberty in the sands of Carolina." More disconcerting, he had forgotten his "breeches" and could not find a tailor to make another pair. So the chief justice had the "extreme mortification" of presiding at court "without that important article of dress." As always, he looked forward to the return to Richmond and the "pleasure of seeing you & our dear children."

When the Supreme Court began hearing argument in *Marbury* v. *Madison* on February 9, 1803, little evidence suggested that this case would become one of the most important and the most controversial in the Court's history—and the fulcrum for divergent interpretations of the judicial actions of John Marshall. The chief justice did not arrive until the day after the opening of the term on February 7. Cushing was ill and missed the entire argument. Paterson missed the first day, and Moore did not arrive until the last day of testimony on February 12. The disappointments of the preceding fourteen months had dashed Federalist hopes of using the judiciary to cancel the Repeal Act. Jefferson and Madison—more concerned with negotiations leading to the Louisiana Purchase than with arguing a "moot" case—did not even present the government side of the case. Even as a challenge to executive power, the case had lost its significance. In February 1803 Federalist senators had chosen new ground and launched an attack on Jefferson's foreign policy.

Marshall knew that the question of the Court's authority and of its relation to the other branches of government remained unanswered. He knew also that the *Marbury* case presented a unique opportunity to address that question. In addition to its other weaknesses, the Court—as distinct from the judiciary system—suffered from lack of publicity about its decisions. Reporting was unsystematic, and public information about the Court's actions depended upon reliable newspaper accounts. Because the press had riveted public attention to the judiciary since the closing days of the Adams administration, and because the *Marbury* case had long been a source of controversy, the chance existed for a full reporting of this opinion. Marshall devoted his decision of February 24 to a full exposition of the principles of good government.

The opinion answered three questions. Was Marbury entitled to his commission? Yes, said Marshall. Marbury, once appointed and confirmed, had a vested right in the office for the term fixed by statute. The president had no discretionary removal power, and the law required the secretary of state to seal and deliver the commission. Marbury, then, had sustained injury. Was he entitled to a remedy? For Marshall the "very essence of civil liberty" required that every individual have the right to "claim protection of the laws whenever he receives an injury." It was an axiom of Anglo-American law that "every right, when withheld, must have a remedy." The government of the United States, Marshall said, "has been emphatically termed a government of laws, and not of men. It will certainly cease to deserve this high appellation if the laws furnish no remedy for the violation of a vested legal right." And, he

Signature (handwritten margin note)

emphasized, "the question, whether a right has vested or not, is, in its nature, judicial." Was the remedy a writ of mandamus issuing from the Supreme Court? No! Marshall ruled that Section 13 of the 1789 Judiciary Act, which authorized such writs, was unconstitutional because Congress did not have the power to alter the original jurisdiction of the Supreme Court contained in Article III of the Constitution. The Constitution, he declared in a proclamation of judicial review, is "fundamental and paramount law," and it is "emphatically the province and duty of the judicial department to say what the law is."

Marshall could have first denied the Court's jurisdiction. But reversing the order of questions enabled him to scold the president for disobeying the laws. Then, by denying Marbury the writ, he gave the Republicans what they wanted—but he did so through an assertion of judicial review. Jefferson could do nothing about a decision that in its outcome was favorable.

Politics unquestionably dictated the decision and the opinion. That fact, however, does not mean that Marshall engaged in partisan sniping. The relation of the judiciary to the other branches was a serious political-constitutional problem. Marshall sought to establish "the authoritative place of a liberal Constitution kept authentic by the courts." Viewed in this light, *Marbury* v. *Madison* outlined his plan for preserving limited government against the inroads of an ever more powerful democracy.

The Constitution drafted by the enlightened statesmen at the Philadelphia Convention and ratified by the best talents in the several states at their conventions in 1788 was the product of an aristocracy natural to John Marshall. "The people" had "an original right to establish, for their future government, such principles as, in their opinion, shall most conduce to their own happiness." They had done so in 1787 and 1788. "The exercise of this original right is a very great exertion; nor can it, nor ought it to be frequently repeated. Those principles, therefore, are deemed fundamental" and "are designed to be permanent." The election of 1800 had jeopardized those principles, and Marshall knew that the Court alone could not safeguard them.

Therefore, Marshall shaped his opinion—and used the case—to enunciate fundamental principles. An initial invalidation of Section 13 would have prevented the reminder that the law obliged the president to act in certain cases. Similarly, his forced construction of Section 13 enabled Marshall to assert limits to legislative power in general and over the Court in particular. The Court would review executive and legislative actions to preserve the individual liberties guaranteed by the Constitution. On this and earlier occasions he had admitted a right of the other branches to judge certain categories of constitutional questions. "Questions, in their nature political," he said, "or which are, by the constitution and laws, submitted to the executive [and legislative], can never be made in this court." He did, though, reserve to the Court the final power to determine in individual cases which questions were "political" and which the Court could review.

The task Marshall had set for the Court in 1801 required high judicial statesmanship. His arguments and attitudes had not changed since 1788. At the close of the Virginia Convention he had argued that if Congress went "beyond the delegated powers" to make a law not warranted by the Constitution, the judges would declare it void. "To what quarter will you look for protection from an infringement of the constitution, if you will not give the power to the judiciary?" Marshall had asked the delegates.

Jefferson and the moderate Republicans were unperturbed by Marshall's exercise of judicial review. The Court had reviewed a law pertaining only to the judiciary. That action fit perfectly with the Republican view that each branch was competent to decide constitutional questions "in their own spheres of action."

Six days after *Marbury*, the Court gave its opinion in *Stuart* v. *Laird*, which involved the constitutionality of the Repeal Act. On that issue Republicans had resolved to make no compromise. Marshall did not participate in the decision, because he had presided on circuit in December. He was not surprised, however, when Paterson delivered the Court's opinion upholding the act. Like *Marbury*, this decision was a Court opinion, and it conformed exactly to what the justices had decided in their conference in the spring of 1802. The Court, though political, would not be a tool for partisan purposes—even if that meant letting go by default the constitutional question of Congress's power to remove judges by eliminating the office. The question, said Paterson, was at rest and ought not be disturbed. The Court had weathered the partisan storm and kept its independence intact. "The weight of your authority," said the Republican *Aurora*, "then calmed the tumult of faction, and you stood, as you must continue to stand, a star of the first magnitude."

Although moderates had prevented a war on the judiciary, radical Republicans had talked about impeachment for some time. Two incidents in 1803 whipped up the smoldering fires of the judiciary controversy.

In February Jefferson sent the House of Representatives evidence that John Pickering, federal district judge in New Hampshire, was guilty of drunkenness and profanity while on the bench. Less than a month later the House voted to impeach Pickering for malfeasance and general unfitness for office. In March 1804 the Senate convicted this pathetic figure; he was also hopelessly insane. In May 1803 Justice Chase, still fuming over the Repeal Act, delivered a tirade against mobocracy and the administration to a Baltimore grand jury. This latest outburst from the most rabid partisan on the Federalist bench was too much even for moderate Republicans. On the very day the Senate convicted Pickering, the House passed a resolution impeaching Chase, who was ultimately acquitted after a spectacular trial in February 1805.

Both cases were hopelessly mired in contemporary politics. Pickering's erratic behavior had long been an issue in New Hampshire politics. He had been appointed to the federal bench to remove him from the state court. Federalists themselves had used a provision of the 1801 Judiciary Act—allowing circuit judges to appoint one of their number to replace an incapacitated judge—to shelve him. Ironically, the Repeal Act had thrust Pickering back into action.

Chase had not only been injudicious; he had violated the law. Overlooking his behavior, Federalists argued that impeachment would eliminate judicial independence. The Constitution, they asserted, required proof of "high crimes and misdemeanors." Neither judge, they maintained, was guilty by that standard. Republicans countered that impeachment was a necessary political inquest without which any administration could fill the courts with judges holding sinecures. Congress could remove judges at its discretion, provided it had the necessary two-thirds majority.

Intense partisanship, especially in the Chase trial, obscured an important constitutional point. Judges held office during good behavior; that requirement necessarily implied removal for bad behavior—a lesser matter than "high crimes and misdemeanors." Nothing in the Constitution prohibited Congress or the judges themselves from initiating procedures to remove judges for misconduct or incapacity. In fact, as Pickering's case demonstrated, the Judiciary Act of 1801 had done just that.

Speculation was rampant that Marshall would be the next to go if Chase were convicted. He wrote his brother that the impeachments were sufficient to "alarm the friends of a pure, and, of course, an independent Judiciary." He expressed the same concern to Chase and added the startling suggestion that granting Congress the power to reverse legal opinions it deemed unsound "would certainly better comport" with the spirit of American government than the constant threat of impeachment. Throughout the contest over the judiciary Marshall had been more concerned with judicial independence than with judicial power.

There is no reason to suspect a Republican vendetta against Marshall. Jefferson thought impeachment "a *bungling way*" of removing judges even before the "bungled" Chase acquittal. He preferred a constitutional amendment to allow the president to remove judges if asked to do so by both houses of Congress. Moreover, no anti-Marshall bias was apparent at the Chase trial.

Three days after Chase's acquittal, Marshall presided at Jefferson's second inauguration. His first four years as chief justice had been stormy but not unproductive. Struggling against great odds he had established the independence of the judiciary. On that inauguration day in 1805 he was also deeply involved with the "least satisfactory" labor of his life— his *Life of George Washington*.

Bushrod Washington had custody of George Washington's papers and asked Marshall to write the book while Washington would serve an editorial function. The massive five-volume literary venture had occupied Marshall and Bushrod Washington since 1800. They had begun negotiating with publishers shortly after the general's death. The first volume, a history of the colonies from settlement to Washington's youth, and the second, taking Washington to the Revolution, appeared in 1804. The next two, covering his military career, came out just after the Chase trial. Marshall was still working on the fifth volume, a history of the Constitution from the Convention in 1787 through Washington's death in 1799.

The work was a disappointment, even though Marshall's $20,000 share of the royalties helped make the final payment on the Fairfax purchase. The deliberate, lackluster style that enhanced judicial opinions proved disastrous in a biography. Washington, the man, never appeared. Washington, the symbol, however, pervaded the work, and that was the purpose of the volumes—to remind Americans of the principles of good government. Marshall's *Washington* was not only a prime source of his principles but also his "most elaborate statement on American politics."

Jefferson certainly read the work that way. He called it a "political diatribe" and a "five-volume libel," and it was the single greatest source of personal antagonism between the two statesmen. Jefferson learned of the venture before a word had been written and believed it would be a Federalist history, which it was. More important, he thought it an electioneering device for the 1804 election, which it was not. He bought each volume as it came out and resented the work even in his last years. He persuaded the poet and diplomat Joel Barlow to write a Republican history. However, Barlow died before completing the work. This led to the compilation of Jefferson's *Anas*, and the lengthy introduction to that personal history was a refutation of Marshall's work.

Marshall, said Jefferson, did not recognize or appreciate the devotion to the betterment of the human condition which inspired the American Revolution and the Republican party. "The sufferings inflicted on endeavors to vindicate the rights of humanity," he said in the *Anas*, "are related with all the frigid insensibility with which a monk would have contemplated the victims of an auto da fe."

VI

Life, Liberty, and Property

1807–1812

THE SCOURGE OF POLITICS lashed Marshall less severely after 1805. With the renewed outbreak of war between England and France, foreign affairs replaced the judiciary as the chief object of Republican concern. Facing the responsibilities of power, the Republicans now became the party of nationalism. The Federalists, demoralized after their defeat in 1804, lapsed into New England parochialism, and talked of states' rights, even of secession. Jefferson and Madison appointments brought a Republican majority to the Supreme Court by 1812, but this majority only complemented Marshall's own nationalism and helped consolidate the gains made during the struggle for judicial independence. Secure as an institution, the Court now turned its attention to the supremacy of national power and the protection of individual liberties. *Fletcher* v. *Peck* (1810) and the treason trial of Aaron Burr in 1807 demonstrated that human liberty, centering on the natural rights to life, liberty, and property, formed the core of Marshall's jurisprudence.

*   *   *

The trial of Aaron Burr was one of the most spectacular trials in American history. It involved the gravest of political crimes and the wildest of partisan recriminations—not to mention a man's very life. Jefferson committed the government's resources to Burr's conviction. Marshall, fearful that the charge of treason might become an instrument of political repression, sought to balance the welfare of the accused with the welfare of society.

The origins of the case extended back through a labyrinth of intrigues, foreign cabals, border disputes, coded letters, betrayals, and, finally, a duel with Alexander Hamilton in 1804, when Burr became an object of mystery and notoriety. When the political prospects of this grandson of Jonathan Edwards were dashed, the hero of the Revolution and vice president of the United States turned to the expansive West to recoup his fortunes. His close collaborator was James Wilkinson, commanding general of the United States army. Fat, glib, and pompous, Wilkinson was also a paid Spanish spy, a master of duplicity. The two men planned to raise a large private army of disgruntled westerners to accomplish their goal of severing Louisiana from the United States. At various times the scheme embraced an invasion of Mexico, an assault on Washington, D.C., and the formation of a new nation out of the states west of the Alleghenies. Upon retiring as vice president, Burr ventured down the Ohio and Mississippi rivers to New Orleans to line up support. Carried away by the enthusiastic response, he talked too much, and rumors flew across the country. By August, while he was still returning overland from New Orleans, the Richmond *Enquirer* and other newspapers began to publish stories of his plot to revolutionize Louisiana.

These rumors could not have escaped the notice of John Marshall. Thomas Ritchie, editor of the *Enquirer,* was a frequent guest at the Marshall house. Furthermore, Marshall's brother-in-law, Joseph H. Daveiss, was the first to call the conspiracy to Jefferson's attention. From January to August 1806 the United States district attorney for Kentucky relayed details of the schemes to the president and specifically named

Burr among the conspirators. Noting the Republican names and Daveiss's Federalism, Jefferson dismissed the information as partisan intrigue designed to embarrass the administration. That summer Daveiss and his brother-in-law Humphrey Marshall underwrote the *Western World,* a Kentucky newspaper devoted to chronicling the conspiracy.

Unperturbed by the commotion, Burr went West again in the summer of 1806. His financial mainstay, a renegade Irishman named Harman Blennerhassett, owned an island in the Ohio River within the bounds of Wood County, Virginia. Burr arranged for his forces to rendezvous at this spot, sent a coded letter to Wilkinson sketching his plans, and went on to Lexington to recruit men and boats for the expedition. Then his plans went awry.

Burr's notoriety alarmed his partner Wilkinson. In October the wily realist sent Jefferson a decoded copy of Burr's letter and a carefully worded note exposing the conspiracy—with no mention of his own involvement. On November 27, two days after receiving the letter, Jefferson issued a proclamation urging all public officials to bring the conspirators to punishment. In Kentucky, Daveiss acted on his own authority and haled Burr into court three times for organizing an expedition against Spanish territory. Each case failed for lack of evidence. In December Blennerhassett and thirty or forty men escaped the island and narrowly missed capture by a party of Ohio militiamen. Burr joined them at the mouth of the Cumberland, and the small force headed toward New Orleans.

Wilkinson had gone to New Orleans in November to save the city. Warning of imminent invasion, he proclaimed martial law, over the objection of the territorial governor. Then he summarily arrested a number of his erstwhile colleagues, defied writs of habeas corpus, and shipped his cohorts in chains to Washington. In January 1807 Burr surrendered his motley force of nine boats and about one hundred men to authorities in the Mississippi Territory, where a grand jury refused to indict him. When he learned that Wilkinson had offered a $5,000 reward for his capture and had sent troops to bring him to New Orleans for a court martial, Burr fled, only to be captured in Alabama and brought to Richmond on March 26, 1807.

Jefferson briefly noted these escapades in his December message to Congress, with no mention of Burr and no hint of treason. Congress felt entitled to more information. On January 22, 1807, in response to a House demand for details, Jefferson informed Congress that little "formal and legal evidence" was available and that "it was difficult to sift out the real facts" from the conjecture, rumor, and suspicion. Then, with remarkable ease, he sifted the facts through the sieve of Wilkinson's evidence. Clearly, he said, Burr commanded a military enterprise to seize New Orleans and use it as a base to detach the states west of the Alleghenies and to conquer Mexico. Burr planned nothing less than "the severance of the Union," and Jefferson proclaimed him a traitor whose "guilt is placed beyond all question." The private Jefferson had broken through the usually circumspect public posture. The question of Burr's guilt or innocence receded; public attention focused on the author of the Declaration of Independence, who had publicly condemned a man not yet tried by a jury.

Marshall then entered the Burr drama. The circuit court for the District of Columbia committed for treason Erick Bollman and Samuel Swartwout, two of Wilkinson's prisoners. William Cranch, the lone Federalist judge, opposed the commitment. "Dangerous precedents occur in dangerous times," he said. With the public mind agitated, it was "the duty of the judiciary calmly to poise the scales of justice, unmoved by the armed power, undisturbed by the clamor of the multitude." The two defendants appealed to the Supreme Court for a writ of habeas corpus.

Ex parte Bollman and Swartwout (1807) raised some of the same questions as did the *Marbury* case. Did the Court have the authority to issue the writ? In an expansive reading of the 1789 Judiciary Act, Marshall answered affirmatively for the majority, although Justice William Johnson, Jefferson's first appointment to the Court, wrote a spirited dissent. The second question, whether the defendants were entitled to the writ, brought no dissent. Marshall spoke for a unanimous majority and ruled the evidence insufficient to justify commitment and trial for treason.

At the crux of the *Bollman* decision was the chief justice's searching explanation of the American law of treason. Much of the opinion was characteristically obiter dicta (saying more than was necessary to a decision), but for a long time American constitutional law rested largely on Marshall's dicta. Constitutional principles needed clarification—especially on the crime of treason, which could so "excite and agitate the passions of men." Wilkinson's heavy-handed disregard for civil authority and Jefferson's indiscretions only confirmed this necessity. And Marshall's clarification remained the basis of the American law on treason until World War II.

He based the opinion solely on the Constitution. The framers, he noted, had "defined and limited" treason and "with jealous circumspection attempted to protect their limitation." They had provided that no person could be convicted without the testimony of two witnesses to the "overt act" or a confession in open court. Article III, section 3 of the Constitution specified that treason consisted "only in levying war" against the United States or "adhering to their enemies by giving them aid and comfort." Affidavits by Wilkinson and William Eaton, another sometime conspirator, provided the required testimony. But what constituted "levying war"? Marshall said that to establish such a fact a body of men had to have "actually assembled, for the purpose of effecting by force a treasonable purpose." Conspiracy to commit treason, no matter how heinous, was not treason without the overt act. Congress could legislate a crime of conspiracy, but the Constitution strictly

defined treason. It was "more consonant to the principles of
our constitution, that the crime of treason should not be extended by construction to doubtful cases."

Burr's trial began on March 30, 1807, lasted seven months,
and produced a spectacular display of partisan fireworks. Jefferson had moved swiftly when he learned that Burr was
widely supported by northern Federalists, whose secessionist
machinations had become a vexing irritant. Convinced that
he was above party, that the Republican party was synonymous
with the nation, the president determined to crush this partisan threat to Union.

Marshall returned to Richmond late in March to find Burr
confined under guard in a room at the Eagle Tavern. He
promptly issued a warrant ordering the prisoner's appearance
before the circuit court. At noon on March 30 Burr came
before Marshall in a closed room in the tavern for a preliminary hearing to determine whether he should be released on
bail. United States District Attorney George Hay repeated his
motion to commit Burr on charges of treason and misdemeanor; the defense argued insufficient evidence for treason
and urged bail on the misdemeanor. Marshall said he would
give his opinion the next day. Wisely, he decided to write his
opinions in this case "to prevent any misrepresentations."

On April 1, Marshall delivered the first of many opinions
in the Burr trial. Carefully, he explained that before the court
would hold the prisoner for the grand jury the government
would have to "furnish good reason to believe" that Burr had
committed the crimes with which he had been charged. The
"hand of malignity" could not "grasp any individual against
whom its hate may be directed." The evidence was the same
as in the *Bollman* case. So was Marshall's conclusion. Probable
cause could be found for holding Burr for planning to invade
Mexico, but only a suspicion of treason existed. The overt act,
he chided the prosecution, must be proved. "Months have
elapsed since the fact did occur, if it ever occurred. More than
five weeks have elapsed since the . . . supreme court has de-

clared the necessity of proving the fact, if it exists. Why is it not proved?" Marshall refused to commit Burr for treason and set bail at $10,000 for the misdemeanor.

Jefferson was furious. Even Republicans in Congress had questioned his support of Wilkinson. Now, twice in five weeks, Federalist judges had ruled against his evidence. "It is unfortunate," he wrote the day after Marshall's decision, "that federalism is still predominant in our judiciary," because the courts could "baffle" the elected branches. Jefferson believed that Marshall had been unreasonable in demanding the presentation of evidence on such short notice. Bollman and Swartwout, however, had been taken in December, as had Blennerhassett's men, and that was enough time to procure the evidence, "if it existed." Marshall had also allowed the prosecution to collect proof and seek indictment for treason in May. Jefferson set his mind to do so.

The president, who had publicly proclaimed Burr's guilt, fumed about "tricks of the judges" and the perversion of "all the principles of law." Jefferson replaced probable cause with the "probable ground" furnished by the "universal belief or rumor" of Burr's guilt. He talked of a constitutional amendment to render the judiciary less independent of the elected branches and of "the common sense of the nation." In February he defended Wilkinson's actions on the grounds that good officers had to go beyond the "strict line of the law" when the public good required it.

A contretemps confirmed Jefferson's suspicions, though not Marshall's partisanship. During the three weeks Burr was free on bail Marshall attended a dinner given by John Wickham, an old friend from the Quoit Club and leader of the Richmond bar, to whom Marshall had turned over his practice in 1797. Wickham was not only one of Burr's lawyers but a Burr partisan—and Burr was at the dinner! Marshall did not know of this situation in advance. Few attributed "any corrupt motive" to the chief justice, but most felt that he was "surely guilty of an unpardonable breach of prudence and decorum."

In a case with so many political overtones, the spectacle of the judge and the accused dining together just before the trial seemed more than indiscretion.

It was apparent when the court convened on May 22 that Marshall would have his hands full. An astute lawyer in his own right, Burr assumed direction of his defense and had assembled a dazzling array of legal talent to assist him. Joining Wickham were Edmund Randolph and Charles Lee, former attorneys general of the United States; Luther Martin, the eloquent, inebriate, anti-Jeffersonian leader of the Maryland bar; and two able young Richmond trial lawyers. Loyal and diligent George Hay directed the prosecution. Jefferson had appropriated over $11,000 (unauthorized by Congress) to retain counsel to assist Hay, but Burr had already skimmed the cream. Hay's ablest associate was William Wirt, young, learned, and at the threshold of a brilliant legal career. Alexander McRae, the forceful but tactless lieutenant governor of Virginia, also assisted. "There never was such a trial since the beginning of the world to this day," Hay complained to Jefferson.

Burr seized the initiative the first day. He immediately challenged the impartiality of jurors such as William Branch Giles, who had publicly proclaimed his guilt. After much wrangling and numerous exceptions, Marshall empaneled a grand jury of sixteen—fourteen Republicans, many close friends of Jefferson, and only two Federalists. John Randolph, a leader of the Republican opposition to Jefferson but bitterly opposed to Burr, was foreman. Burr then asked Marshall to instruct the jury on the admissibility of evidence he expected Hay to introduce. When Hay attempted to block this move Burr began an anti-administration tirade. Marshall intervened and adjourned the court to allow opposing counsel time to prepare "further discussions." The next day brought only impassioned recriminations.

On Monday, May 25, the grand jury assembled to hear evidence. Hay, however, was not yet ready—Wilkinson, his star witness, was absent. Embarrassed, Hay sought delay by asking the court to imprison Burr on a charge of treason. Otherwise, he argued, Burr was likely to jump bail to avoid a confrontation with the general. The ensuing debate caught Marshall in a partisan crossfire. If he stopped Hay, critics would accuse him of favoring Burr. If he did not, it would appear that the court had been intimidated. He allowed Hay to take testimony but repeatedly reminded him of the necessity to prove the act as well as the intent to commit treason. All the while, the grand jury adjourned from day to day awaiting Wilkinson's appearance. Marshall recessed the court for a week so the jurors, as Washington Irving said, "might go home, see their wives, get their clothes washed, and flog their negroes."

Wilkinson still had not appeared when the proceedings resumed on June 9. Burr asked the court to issue a subpoena duces tecum to the president requiring the delivery of the letter and other papers he had received from Wilkinson on October 21. Dumbfounded at this bold attack on the administration, Hay argued that the materiality of the evidence in this case had not been shown but did not challenge the authority of the court to issue a subpoena to the president. Marshall called for argument and after three days of purple oratory delivered his opinion awarding the subpoena.

Characteristically, Marshall used the occasion to clarify "sound legal principles." The judiciary had the power to compel testimony even from the president. But the president was not an ordinary citizen and might have sufficient grounds for refusing to produce a particular paper. The court would weigh the president's reasons against the claims of the accused. In brief, materiality to the defense might overrule presidential objections, and the court would be the final judge.

The subpoena business produced a flurry of letters between Hay and Jefferson in which the president denied the power of the court to compel his attendance. But Marshall had not ordered Jefferson to appear—only to supply papers. Jefferson complied. On June 12, before Marshall's opinion, he stated his readiness "voluntarily to furnish on all occasions, whatever the purposes of justice may require." Marshall did not insist on making the letters public. He did insist that the papers be delivered to the court for its determination whether the information was material to the defense. Jefferson did not claim executive privilege. Both he and Hay were willing to let the court decide materiality.

Wilkinson's arrival on the day of Marshall's opinion pushed the subpoena into the background. He was sworn in on June 15 and, with other witnesses, was questioned before the grand jury for much of the week. The star witness, forced to make damaging admissions, proved as embarrassing in person as in absentia. On June 24 the grand jury nevertheless indicted Burr for treason, charging that on December 10, 1806, he had levied war against the United States on Blennerhassett's Island, and for the misdemeanor of organizing an expedition against Spanish territory. Seven of the sixteen jurymen also voted to indict Wilkinson, whom Randolph called a "mammoth of iniquity" and a villain "from the bark to the very core." Burr pleaded innocent and was sent to the new state penitentiary outside Richmond to await trial. Marshall adjourned the court to August 3.

The chief justice believed treason trials on other circuits were likely, and he wanted the Supreme Court justices to act in concert. Pursuing consensus as he had in 1802, Marshall sought the opinion of his fellow justices on the *Bollman* decision, which he believed should control the Burr case. Jefferson was also uneasy. In mid-July, he wrote that although "there is not a man in the U.S. who is not satisfied of [Burr's] guilt, such are the jealous provisions of our laws in favor of the accused, and against the accuser, that I question if he can be convicted."

Burr's trial lasted from August 3 to September 1 and brought no surprises. It took two weeks to empanel a jury. Then, in the sweltering heat, counsel harangued each other and the crowded hall. No new questions arose, only weeks of oratory. Burr and his associates prosecuted the administration; Hay, despite Wirt's eloquence, watched his case crumble.

The central problem was Marshall's *Bollman* ruling. Marshall had reminded Hay of that ruling during the hearing to commit Burr and again during the grand jury proceedings. Hay, for whatever reason, did not get the message. His 140 witnesses could testify only to Burr's intentions. Marshall had many times ruled that intentions must be manifest in deeds proved by two witnesses.

Hay's opening statement aimed to prove that Burr had gathered men at Blennerhassett's Island but denied that force must be employed to commit treason. Admitting that Burr was not present on the island, he argued for a constructive presence. His witnesses did little more than establish the presence of armed men on the island—not an exceptional circumstance on the frontier. Burr's counsel argued that physical presence was required by the Constitution. The desperate Hay insisted that the question was not where the accused was when the act was committed but whether he had procured it or had a part in it. He proposed to establish Burr's procurement through Wilkinson's testimony. This proposal touched off a ten-day display of legal pyrotechnics.

After patiently allowing counsel to run their course, Marshall finally read his opinion on August 31. It took him three hours to read the rambling, repetitious twenty-five thousand words that became the authoritative exposition of the American law of treason. Basically, Marshall addressed the questions he had taken up in *Bollman:* What constituted "levying war," and were all parties to treason principals? "War," he stated, "could not be levied without the employment and exhibition of force." The Constitution did not admit the doctrine of constructive treason. Not all who participated were principals—only all who "performed a part" in the perpetration of war to which two witnesses could testify. What concerned Marshall was the difference between "performing a part" and conspiracy not matched by deeds. His strict interpretation of the Constitution's provisions and his firmness on evidence accorded perfectly with the intent of the framers. Treason lay beyond partisan politics. Burr's acquittal was inevitable.

Marshall's concluding statement accurately forecast his ruling's reception. "That this court dares not usurp power is most true," he said. "That this court dares not shrink from its duty is not less true. . . . No man is desirous of becoming the peculiar subject of calumny." Having instructed the jury on the law, Marshall asked them to apply it to the facts in the case. Next morning Edward Carrington, jury foreman and Marshall's brother-in-law, announced, "Burr is not proved to be guilty by any evidence submitted to us. We therefore find him not guilty."

The Burr case occupied six more weeks of Marshall's time. Burr's indictment for the misdemeanor of planning an expedition against Spanish territory also specified Blennerhassett's Island, and Hay wanted to quash it. Marshall ruled that the case must go to the jury. After deliberating only half an hour, that jury too returned a verdict of "not guilty." The case then simply faded away. The repercussions did not.

Jefferson interpreted Marshall's opinions as a political decision. He wrote Hay that the outcome had been planned from the beginning—to clear Burr and prevent the evidence from reaching the public. As if to confirm this partisan judgment, the fifth volume of Marshall's *Washington* and a scathing Daveiss attack on President Jefferson's misconduct appeared simultaneously. "We have no law but the will of the judge," Jefferson told a friend, and any attempt to improve the law would only provide "new materials for sophistry." He called the problem to the attention of a special session of Congress, which had convened in late October to deal with deteriorating relations with Britain.

The Burr trial scarred everyone connected with it. Burr retired to a life of exile and dissipation. Jefferson's intemperate prosecution tarnished his libertarianism. Marshall had gone out of his way to avoid a head-on clash with the president and had allowed the prosecution full rein. Yet after the decision he, not Jefferson, was hanged in effigy, pilloried in the press, and accused of bending the law to partisan ends.

The appearance of three Republicans on the Court by 1807 signaled the end of the old Federalist majority. The bold, eloquent, and assertive William Johnson of South Carolina had replaced Moore in 1804. Connected to commercial interests in Charleston, Johnson was an economic nationalist who differed from Marshall principally in his more restrained view of the judicial function and in his willingness to allow Congress and the states a freer hand. When Paterson died in 1806, Jefferson appointed Henry Brockholst Livingston of New York. Livingston's background as a member of one of New York's most prominent families and as a colleague of Chancellor James Kent on the New York Supreme Court pointed to a fundamental harmony with Marshall's views. Thomas Todd of Kentucky, an expert in land title cases who came to the Bench in 1807 when Congress increased the number of justices to seven, also shared Marshall's concern for property and Union.

These Republicans generally supported Marshall's management of the Court—some said they succumbed to the "leprosy of the Bench." Despite occasional dissents, particularly by Johnson, and seriatim opinions, the Court continued to speak with one voice, usually Marshall's. (Between 1801 and 1835 the chief justice wrote 519 of the Court's 1106 opinions and 36 of the 62 involving constitutional questions.) During 1809 and 1810 the Court displayed its consensus on maintaining national authority against state challenges and on the protection of individual rights, met little executive resistance, and further consolidated judicial power.

The problem of state power assumed ominous proportions during the closing years of Jefferson's second administration and the early years of Madison's term. The new threat resulted from the convergence of two totally unconnected movements:

one, ironically, by New England Federalists; the other by Pennsylvania. Federalists, upset by Jefferson's awkward handling of the threat to American commerce posed by the bitter struggle between Napoleon and Britain, particulary objected to the 1807 embargo. In their view, this embargo would ruin the New England economy and impel the United States to war with Britain. Marshall shared this opinion, but he would not abide the Federalists' open resistance to the law. When a lower federal court upheld the constitutionality of the embargo, enraged Federalists used their state legislatures to register constitutional objections as had the Virginia Republicans of 1798.

A Pennsylvania case gave the Supreme Court an opportunity to strike a blow against both movements. *United States* v. *Peters* (1809) originated during the Revolution when the Committee of Appeals of the Continental Congress overruled a Pennsylvania court decision on the proceeds from the sale of a captured ship, and the state refused to accede. At length in 1803 federal District Judge Richard Peters upheld the committee's ruling. The state legislature in turn resolved that Peters had usurped jurisdiction and ordered the governor to use the militia to protect Pennsylvania's right. In 1808 the Supreme Court ordered Peters to enforce his decision. It would not allow a state to interpret federal law. "If the legislatures of the several states may, at will, annul the judgments of the courts of the United States," Marshall held, "the constitution itself becomes a mockery, and the nation is deprived of the means of enforcing its laws by the instrumentality of its own tribunals."

Marshall's decision did not end the resistance. The governor of Pennsylvania called out the militia, while the legislature denied the Court's authority to decide a question of states' rights and called for a constitutional amendment to create an impartial tribunal to settle such disputes. The threat of armed conflict receded when the new president, James Madison, informed the governor that the executive branch would enforce Court decrees no matter how determined the resistance. Eleven states condemned Pennsylvania's defiance of federal court authority; even Virginia recognized that the Supreme Court was, above any other tribunal, "more eminently qualified from their habits and duties, from the mode of their selection, and from the tenure of their offices" to decide such disputes impartially.

United States v. *Peters* also implied that protection of the individual's acquisitive "interest," or his property right, was the dynamic of national growth. The states had some power over economic development. But when state and individual economic interests clashed, the Supreme Court would make the final choice. National supremacy and economic policy went hand in hand.

Fletcher v. *Peck* (1810), involving one of the great land speculation schemes, had been the subject of bitter controversy for nearly fifteen years. In 1795 four land companies induced the Georgia legislature through bribes to sell thirty-five million acres along the Yazoo River for a trifling half million dollars. Angry over the fraud, the indignant Georgians threw the rascals out. In 1796 a new legislature repealed the 1795 grant. But the lands had already been resold to innocent third parties. One, the New England Mississippi Land Company, purchased over eleven million acres on the day of the repeal. The title to this huge tract ultimately came before Marshall and the Supreme Court.

A pamphlet by Representative Robert Goodloe Harper, prominent South Carolina Federalist, cogently set forth the New England Mississippi Land Company's argument against repeal. Purely and simply, the original sale was a contract; and one party to a contract, even the government, could not exempt himself from its obligations. An appendix quoted a legal opinion of Alexander Hamilton. "Every grant from one to another," said Hamilton, "whether the grantor be a state or an individual, is virtually a contract." Article I, section 10 of the Constitution prohibited the states from passing any law impairing the obligation of contract. Therefore, "taking the terms of the constitution in their large sense, and giving them effect according to the general spirit and policy of the provisions," Hamilton concluded that the 1796 repeal was void and that courts of the United States would "be likely to pronounce it so."

The company had considered an appeal to the federal court from the date of the repeal. But the Eleventh Amendment of 1798 had prevented a suit against Georgia without her consent. To overcome the obstacles the company took advantage of a constitutional provision giving federal courts jurisdiction over suits between citizens of different states. In 1803 John Peck, a Boston director of the company, sold a portion of his land to Robert Fletcher, an accomplished New Hampshire speculator with no formal link to the Yazoo scheme. Fletcher then promptly sued Peck in the United States circuit court in Massachusetts for selling land that he did not rightfully possess. Fletcher claimed that the repeal act had invalidated Peck's title and thus sought a direct ruling on it.

Beyond doubt this suit was collusive, arranged for the benefit of the New England Mississippi Land Company and lacking every quality of an adversary proceeding. Lawyers in the case included speculators, Yazoo claimants, and Harper. Both parties agreed to a continuance each year from 1803 to 1806 while some chance remained of a compromise in Congress. Only when that hope vanished did the trial begin. In the fall of 1807 the circuit court upheld Peck's title, and Fletcher appealed to the Supreme Court on a writ of error. After argument in 1809, the Court continued the case to the 1810 term.

On March 16, 1810, Marshall announced the Court's decision that the Georgia repeal act was invalid because it violated both natural law and the contract clause of the Constitution. This decision went to the heart of his political principles and of his view of the Union. The first in a line of contract clause cases and the first in which the Court invalidated a state law because it conflicted with the Constitution, the decision was also controversial because it seemed to countenance fraud and collusive suits and to protect land speculators from public wrath.

The right to acquire property was, in Marshall's view, almost as important as life itself. He had devoted a large portion of his public life to the preservation of that right from infringement by state legislatures. Because the Constitution "was understood to prohibit all laws impairing the obligation of contracts," he wrote in the fifth volume of his *Washington,* it had "restored that confidence which is essential to the internal prosperity of nations." To a friend in 1809 he wrote that "the interference of the legislature in the management of our private affairs" was "dangerous and unwise. I have always thought so and I still think so." His own legal problems with the Fairfax lands, still unsettled, reinforced these long-standing convictions.

Marshall admitted that Georgia had the power to make the original grant in 1795. That "corruption" and "impure motives should contribute to the passage of a law," he thought was "most deeply to be deplored." But, he continued, it would be "indecent in the extreme, upon a private contract between two individuals, to enter into an inquiry respecting the corruption of the sovereign power of a state." The Court was neither willing nor able to judge motives or to decide how much corruption it would take to invalidate a statute. The people of Georgia had done so in the only way possible—at the polls.

The question of whether state legislatures could "annihilate" the property rights of innocent third parties was one the Court could address. By conveying land Georgia had vested "absolute rights," Marshall said, and only by a naked assertion of absolute legislative power could such rights be recalled. The chief justice would not admit such plenary power in the legislature. The nature of society and of government prescribed some limits to legislative power; and the property of an individual, fairly and honestly acquired, could not be seized without compensation. Natural law, or what Marshall called "certain great principles of justice, whose authority is universally acknowledged," would void such power even if Georgia were an independent sovereign state. But Georgia was a member of the Union, bound by the Constitution, which imposed restrictions on the state legislatures.

"A contract is a compact between two or more parties," he said, "and is either executory or executed." Both imposed binding obligations: the former to do something; the latter not to undo what had been done. A grant was an executed contract, and the Constitution did not distinguish between public and private grants. The Georgia repeal act's interference with the grant was, then, voided "either by the general principles . . . common to our free institutions, or by the particular provisions of the Constitution."

The framers of the Constitution did not intend the contract clause to embrace anything other than agreements between private individuals. But Marshall stretched its meaning. Although nothing in the Constitution affirmed his interpretation, nothing denied it. His opinion addressed the "general principles" of that document, and he knew the framers had intended the Constitution to limit state power over individual rights to life, liberty, and property.

The justices offered no dissents. Cushing and Chase were absent. Johnson wrote a concurring opinion which supported the majority on natural law grounds but disagreed with Marshall's application of the contract clause. He predicted that the Court would find "extreme difficulty" drawing the line or defining the words "obligation of contract." He also did not want to restrict constitutionally, in favor of property rights, the states' power to act in the general welfare. On the main point Johnson and Marshall (and thus the whole Court) agreed. Once property is granted to a man, said Johnson, it "becomes intimately blended with his existence, as essentially as the blood that circulates through his system."

Fletcher v. *Peck* did not end the Yazoo controversy, which dragged on to 1814 when Congress finally passed compensatory legislation. It did cap the development of the doctrines first stated in *Marbury,* when Marshall proclaimed the primacy of the Constitution and defended an independent judiciary as necessary to protect the property, or vested, rights of individuals. By 1810 the Court was not only independent but also a sturdy and respected branch of the national government. Its attention focused on preserving the Constitution as the bulwark of individual liberties, the "bill of rights" for liberal Americans. And Marshall, writing most of the opinions, performed much as an Old Testament prophet—reminding his people of their social values and warning of the dangers likely to follow the abandonment of those principles.

Cushing's death in September 1810 left the Court evenly divided between Federalists and Republicans. President Madison's problem was to find a suitable New England Republican, preferably from Massachusetts, willing to fill the empty position. Jefferson, now in retirement at Monticello, warned Madison that it would be difficult to find someone with a character strong enough to preserve his independence on the Bench with Marshall. The chief justice's leadership, Jefferson told the president, displayed "cunning and sophistry" and a "rancorous hatred" of Republican government. "His twistifications of the law in the case of Marbury, in that of Burr, and the late Yazoo case, show how dextrously he can reconcile law to his personal biases."

Chase died while Madison was still searching for a Cushing replacement. In November 1811 the president appointed Joseph Story of Massachusetts and Gabriel Duval of Maryland.

Senate confirmation of these appointments restored the full Court for the 1812 term, and no other change would occur for eleven years. Duval served without distinction for almost a quarter of a century; Story, until death in 1845. Ambitious and erudite, Story became one of the leading jurists of the nineteenth century—a founding father of the

Harvard Law School and the author of numerous legal trea-
tises. He also became Marshall's close friend and colleague.
He had opposed the embargo and quickly revealed a concern
for judicial supremacy, the Union, and property rights that
surpassed that of the chief justice. Duval and Story together
with Marshall, Washington, Johnson, Livingston, and Todd
constituted the Marshall Court.

The chief justice was in his prime. His robust health, full
shock of hair, and "twinkling" black eyes belied his fifty-seven
years. In 1812, he led a surveying expedition into the wilderness of western Virginia to determine which rivers could
be made navigable to open trade with the West. As always, his
plain manners and drawling, familiar conversation left their
imprint. "I love his laugh,—it is too hearty for an intriguer,"
Story wrote. "His good temper and unwearied patience are
equally agreeable on the bench and in the study." Most impressive, though, was his ability to examine the "intricacies"
of a problem with "calm and persevering circumspection" and
then to unravel the "mysteries with irresistible acuteness."

VII

The Marshall Court

1812–1823

MARSHALL'S JUDICIAL CAREER reached its pinnacle between 1812 and 1823, a time of relative stability on the Court and of tumultuous growth for the nation. The War of 1812 stimulated business expansion, a pell-mell westward movement, and pressure for a vigorous national government. Exuberant postwar nationalism turned the Republicans into champions of economic nationalism. Eager to promote unity and economic growth, in 1816 they enacted a protective tariff, chartered the Second Bank of the United States, and sponsored federally financed internal improvements. But the Panic of 1819, an agricultural depression, and the Missouri debates alarmed the agrarian, slaveholding South and provoked arguments going to the very heart of the constitutional system. Virginia resurrected the hoary doctrine of states' rights to meet the challenges of intrusive nationalism. The Marshall Court responded by firmly establishing implied congressional power and the appellate jurisdiction of the Supreme Court and by steadily expanding the contract clause to protect property from state interference.

* * *

The strength of the Marshall Court was its unity. On questions of national power and the Court's jurisdiction the seven justices were emphatically unanimous. When they differed, as they did on the question of concurrent state power, they submerged their differences in the interest of presenting a united front. Jefferson attributed this unity to Marshall's procrustean leadership. "An opinion is huddled up in conclave," he complained in 1820, "perhaps by a majority of one, delivered as if unanimous, and with the silent acquiescence of lazy or timid associates, by a crafty chief judge, who sophisticates the law to his own mind."

Marshall's charm and force of reasoning did exert a powerful influence. As chief justice he enjoyed the advantages of presiding at public sessions, directing the order of business at private sessions, and assigning the writing of opinions. Consensus was an essential part of his judicial philosophy. His method, though, was persuasion, not dominance. When he could not persuade, he allowed the other justices to record their opinions. If he disagreed with the majority, he either kept silent or modified his opinion to achieve unanimity.

The Marshall Court was a collegial body. The justices had common social and economic backgrounds and similar political philosophies. They worked together, roomed together, and took their meals at a common table in the same Capitol Hill boardinghouse. Having left family and friends behind during their two-month sojourn in Washington, they lived a familial—even monastic—existence. "Perfectly familiar and unconstrained" was Story's description in 1812. "Our social hours when undisturbed with the labors of the law, are passed in gay and frank conversation, which at once enlivens and instructs." In these boardinghouse conferences and at their weekly consultation days at Court, Marshall and his colleagues discussed the cases before them in "pleasant and animated exchanges of legal acumen." The Court's opinions, then, were orchestral and not solo performances by Marshall.

One of the first cases of the February 1812 term provided a glimpse of the self-effacing character of the Marshall Court. In *United States* v. *Hudson and Goodwin,* Johnson ended a fifteen-year controversy by denying the Court's power to punish common-law crimes against the United States (those not defined by Congress). Marshall surely disagreed. Even so, he muted his disagreement out of deference to the majority and influenced Story and Washington to follow his example. Story later tried to get the Court to reverse itself and assert common-law jurisdiction. When his effort collapsed after another Johnson opinion in 1816, Marshall and Washington helped him draft legislation to have Congress confer that jurisdiction on the Court. The Congress was not persuaded, although all the justices except Johnson supported the bill. These disagreements and maneuverings, however, never disturbed the unanimity of the Marshall Court on this question.

Also in 1812 the Court unanimously broadened the scope of the contract clause and its own power to broker economic activity in *New Jersey* v. *Wilson*. The New Jersey colonial legislature had granted land to Indians under terms expressly exempting the land from taxation. When the Indians sold the land in 1801, and the state attempted to tax it, the new owners challenged the constitutionality of the tax. The decision was a logical extension of *Fletcher* v. *Peck* and, like that earlier case, reflected Marshall's exclusive concern with protection of individual vested rights and his judicial indifference to the wisdom or unwisdom of public grants. For the second time the Court applied the contract clause to invalidate state action. It would do so again in two great decisions in 1819. New Jersey did not challenge the Court's authority. Virginia was less tractable.

In *Fairfax's Devisee* v. *Hunter's Lessee* (1818), the old case of the Fairfax title and Virginia confiscation legislation, all the passions that land and suspicion of national power evoked in the Old Dominion were brought to the fore. Hunter did not bring his case before the Supreme Court after the 1796 postponement. Instead he brought it before the Virginia Court of Appeals in 1809 and won the following year. Marshall was understandably perturbed. The lands in question were not part of the tract his syndicate had purchased (although they did embrace some of James Marshall's separate purchases), but the chief justice believed the case would "try questions in which we are all interested." Section 25 of the 1789 Judiciary Act allowed appeals from state courts to the Supreme Court in constitutional cases. Marshall urged appeal and expressed a willingness to expedite the matter, although he disqualified himself because of his personal interest.

In March 1813 Story overruled the Virginia court on the ground that the confiscation law violated the Jay treaty. The chief justice and Washington declined to participate. Todd was absent, and Johnson dissented. Only Duval and Livingston joined Story in ordering the Virginia court to reverse its decision. The order touched a raw nerve in Virginia and provoked a controversy over the appellate jurisdiction of the Supreme Court that lasted until 1821.

The presiding judge on the Virginia court was Spencer Roane, who had studied under Wythe with Marshall at William and Mary and was a zealous champion of states' rights. A brilliant jurist, he was also the leader of the Richmond Junto, the powerful machine that dominated political life in Virginia. This formidable opponent of Marshall's judicial nationalism saw in the *Fairfax* case a prime opportunity to strike for states' rights. At his urging the Virginia court heard six days of argument on the question of whether to obey the Supreme Court order. At length, in December 1815, the judges unanimously refused. In a defiant denial of the appellate jurisdiction of the Supreme Court they declared Section 25 of the 1789 Judiciary Act unconstitutional. Roane published their separate opinions in the Richmond *Enquirer,* brought the Junto into the fracas, and obtained the endorsement of Jefferson and Monroe. Almost overnight the land title case became solely a constitutional controversy. The Union would be deprived of its vital force if a state could refuse to obey a Supreme Court order or decide for itself the constitutionality of a federal law. Marshall's brother James immediately appealed the constitutional question to the Supreme Court.

Story met Virginia's challenge with a Marshallian exposition of the Constitution as the organic law of the Union in *Martin v. Hunter's Lessee* (1816). The Constitution, he emphasized, was the creation of the people, not of the states, and was designed to deprive the states of sovereignty. Laying down one of the principal nationalist canons of the Marshall Court, Story declared that the powers of the national government were as extensive as sovereignty and had to be construed generously. Article III mandated that the judicial power of the United States must extend over "all cases" arising from the Constitution, laws, or treaties. Because the vitality of the Union depended upon a uniform interpretation of the Constitution, it followed that the Supreme Court must make the final decision in all constitutional cases whether they originated in state or federal courts. Although Marshall again disqualified himself, he and the other justices endorsed Story's defense of the supervisory role of the Supreme Court. Johnson wrote a concurring opinion allowing the states concurrent judicial power in constitutional cases subject to the discretion of Congress.

The *Martin* case did not settle the controversy. Virginia was indignant. Roane, the Junto, and the *Enquirer* complained bitterly against the decision, and their censures reached a crescendo after Marshall's great nationalizing opinion in *McCulloch v. Maryland* (1819). In 1816 lingering states' rights sentiments evoked some New England sympathy for Virginia's stand. Congress, irritated at the decision, eliminated the justices from a bill to raise the salaries of government officials to keep pace with the postwar inflation.

Great constitutional cases such as *Martin* were exceptional between 1812 and 1816. The Court's work had increased, mostly as a result of the War of 1812. New England's attempts to trade with the enemy, for example, brought nearly twenty cases in which the Court rigidly and unanimously enforced the nonintercourse laws. Numerous complex cases on neutral rights and confiscated property were also heard. On these issues, Marshall and Story parted company. The chief justice believed both international law and the Constitution embodied the great principles of natural justice. He saw international law as a humane and civilized instrument to encourage commerce between nations and to lessen the hardships of war on individuals. Story disagreed and argued in a number of cases that war permitted all kinds of violence in the national interest without discriminating between combatants and noncombatants, belligerents and neutrals. Like Johnson on concurrent state power, the Massachusetts justice felt duty-bound to announce his disagreement formally. Posterity has preferred Story to Marshall on these points.

The end of the war awakened a new sense of national identity and purpose, which flourished during the administration of James Monroe. The Court, once barely an appendage of the government, had established its power to speak authoritatively on the Constitution. Some recognition came in March, when Congress appointed a Court reporter to publish the decisions of the judicial body. And, after years of meeting in makeshift quarters—a tavern on one occasion—the Court settled permanently in a basement courtroom beneath the Senate chamber.

Cases—not rooms, reporters, prestige, or national mood—provide the raw material for judicial fame, and three were building in 1816. In June the New Hampshire legislature erected a state university on the ruins of Dartmouth College. That October a New York creditor sued a debtor in the United States circuit court at Boston. December saw the opening of a branch of the newly chartered Bank of the United States at Baltimore. From these obscure, unconnected events came the three landmark decisions of the 1819 term—"the greatest six weeks in the history of the Court."

In 1819 the Court met for the first time in the new basement room. Small, dark, and inconvenient, the place was more suitable as a dungeon than as the home of the nation's most important tribunal. At eleven o'clock on February 2, Marshall and his associates entered, donned their black robes, and took their seats behind the raised bench while the marshal announced the opening of the Court. Then the chief justice, with three associates sitting on each side, began to read the Court's opinion in *Dartmouth College* v. *Woodward.*

Behind this case lay a tortuous record of personal feuds, sectarian rivalries, and maneuvering that resulted in factions. Dartmouth College was incorporated by a royal charter in 1769. The charter vested control in a self-perpetuating board of trustees, who, in the early years, left the government of the college in the hands of its founder and first president. This tranquil relation disappeared under John Wheelock, second president and son of the founder. Resenting his petulant and self-willed attempts to copy his father's patriarchal administration, the trustees increasingly resisted. The mounting tension exploded into open conflict after the trustees refused to support the Presbyterian president in a quarrel with local Congregationalists. Then, in 1815, Wheelock unwittingly plunged the Dartmouth squabble into the intensely partisan politics of New Hampshire by appealing to the legislature and charging the trustees with hatching a Federalist-Congregationalist conspiracy to subvert popular liberty. Republicans exploited Wheelock's allegations during the state election of 1816. When the trustees fired Wheelock, the Republicans focused their attention on the college's royal charter and warned that the future of popular government in New Hampshire depended upon state control of Dartmouth. After capturing the legislature and the governorship in 1816, the Republicans converted the college into a state university. The new legislature revised the charter by changing the corporation's name to Dartmouth University, enlarging the number of trustees, and making the reorganized institution responsible to the state. Old Wheelock got lost in the shuffle.

Out of this legislation arose the litigation leading to Marshall's 1819 decision. The trustees argued that a charter was a grant of private property rights, that the state constitution prohibited a deprivation of property without a judicial trial, and, because grants were contracts, that the legislation violated the contract clause of the national Constitution. In state court, in order to get a legal decision, they sued William H. Woodward, former secretary–treasurer of the college, who had deserted to the university, for the college records. Expecting the worst, the trustees planned to appeal the contract question to the Supreme Court.

In 1817 the state court confirmed their suspicions in a unanimous decision upholding the legislation. Chief Justice William M. Richardson's opinion addressed the future of the college and the important policy question of state control of corporations. Corporations, he said, were of two classes. Private corporations were created by individuals for their private benefit. Their property stood on the same ground as that of individuals; their charters were contracts protected by the Constitution. Public corporations were created by the state for public purposes. The legislature had the power to regulate them and, Richardson argued, without limitation by the contract clause. Because the education of future generations was a matter of the highest public concern, Dartmouth College was a public corporation and subject to legislative control. The trustees appealed.

The Marshall Court heard argument in the case during the closing days of the 1818 term. Daniel Webster opened for the college on March 10 in one of the most eloquent performances in the Court's history. For four hours he asserted the inviolability of private corporate rights under English common law and the state constitution. Turning to the contract clause, he cited *Fletcher* v. *Peck* and contended that a grant of corporate rights was as much a contract as a grant of land. Everything about him—the flashing eyes, resonant voice, and dramatic gestures—had spellbound the small audience as he paused, then turned to the chief justice and delivered his emotional summation. "It is, sir, as I have said, a small college. And yet *there are those who love it.*" The magnificent performance moved Marshall to tears. University counsel John Holmes and William Wirt could match neither Webster's forensic skill nor his points.

Marshall informed counsel that the Court would give the matter all the consideration due an act of a state legislature but warned that an immediate decision was unlikely. Next morning he announced that some of the justices were divided, and others remained undecided. He continued the case to 1819. When the Court reconvened in 1819, the chief justice pulled an eighteen-page opinion from his sleeve and shattered the university's hopes. Dartmouth College, he said, was a private corporation. Its charter was a contract within the meaning of the Constitution; the New Hampshire legislation was unconstitutional. Story and Washington filed concurring opinions. Todd was absent, and Duval dissented without giving an opinion.

The *Dartmouth College* case climaxed Marshall's expansion of the contract clause into a mighty instrument for the protection of private property rights. In the Yazoo case, he had invalidated the Georgia repeal act on both natural law and constitutional grounds. That ambiguity was gone in 1819. Charters of incorporation, he proclaimed unequivocally, were contracts, "the obligation of which cannot be impaired, without violating the constitution of the United States." No stronger judicial defense of property was put forth in the early nineteenth century.

Chancellor Kent, the eminent New York jurist, called the decision the most important step in securing rights derived from a government grant and in making inviolable the "literary, charitable, religious and commercial institutions of our country." Marshall had immunized private education against state tinkering. His sweeping statement covered the growing number of business corporations and became one of the principal factors in the relation between government and the economy in the nineteenth century.

In 1819 Marshall considered corporations important only as a species of private property. Even the New Hampshire court admitted that *Fletcher* v. *Peck* left little room to doubt that some corporate charters were contracts. But Marshall rejected Justice Richardson's standard that a public interest in the objects, the uses, of private property was sufficient to justify state regulation. Such a standard, he believed, would generate blanket state meddling with private rights. Only by protecting the property, either of individuals or groups of individuals, could the government encourage the productive labor necessary to open the continent and develop the national economy.

The question of what individual rights were involved in this case caused Marshall "real difficulty." His answer was an impressive example of his pragmatic, undoctrinaire approach to the Constitution's fundamental principles. Although "an artificial being, invisible, intangible, and existing only in contemplation of law," the corporation was the instrument for perpetuating the design of the original donors. It stood in their place. Corporate rights, then, were equivalent to private rights. As in *Fletcher* v. *Peck,* the chief justice conceded that the framers did not have such contracts in mind but held that the case came within the spirit of the Constitution. The framers were not so imprudent as to attempt to provide specific rules for problems they could not have foreseen. A constitution had to be flexible and adaptable to circumstances. The language of the Constitution did not exclude this particular interpretation, and the "case being within the words of the rule, must be within its operation likewise." Story, not Marshall, attempted to bring business corporations within the embrace of the decision. His broad application prompted Washington to write a separate opinion limiting the ruling to corporations similar to Dartmouth College.

The *Dartmouth College* decision did not exalt corporate power over the public interest. Marshall clearly did not go that far. Only state legislatures could grant corporate charters, and at the moment of the grant the states were free to set whatever limits they deemed appropriate. Marshall's prohibition on subsequent alteration was an admonition to the states to exercise more caution in their grants. Moreover, he suggested the idea known later as the *state police power* when he said that the framers of the Constitution did not intend to restrain the states in the regulation of civil institutions adopted for internal government. Even Story observed that a state could amend charters by reserving the authority to do so in the original grant, and by the late 1820s such clauses were common. Improvident legislative grants, more than the *Dartmouth College* rule, robbed states of regulatory power. As in *Fletcher* v. *Peck,* Marshall insisted that the wisdom of legislative action was beyond the Court's purview.

Little criticism was made and scant notice was taken of the *Dartmouth College* decision in the press outside New England. The postwar boom had already peaked, and the country was in the throes of the worst depression in its history. A decision affecting the life of a small New England college scarcely seemed relevant to those pressing economic matters.

The second great case of the 1819 term, *Sturges* v. *Crowninshield,* went straight to the vitals of American economic life. At issue was the constitutionality of state bankruptcy laws. The Constitution gave Congress the power to establish uniform bankruptcy laws throughout the nation. The first such federal law in 1800 emphasized fair treatment of creditors, allowed only insolvent merchants to go through bankruptcy, and eliminated imprisonment for debt. But it offered no relief to farmers or to the great mass of noncommercial debtors. Opposition by those parties repealed the law in 1803, and Congress did not enact another until 1841. In the interim the states passed laws as concerned with wiping the debtors' slate clean as with fair treatment of creditors.

New York's bankruptcy law in 1811 relieved insolvent debtors from prior obligations. A fortune-seeker named Richard Crowninshield had borrowed money several weeks before passage of the law and immediately exploited its provisions to obtain a discharge from his obligation. In 1816 his creditor, Josiah Sturges, sued for payment in federal circuit court, arguing that the New York law inpaired the obligation of contract. The circuit judges divided in order to send the case to Washington, D.C. for decision. The ruling of the Supreme Court would have profound economic consequences.

The case raised two important questions. Did the congressional bankruptcy power prohibit state legislation if Congress failed to act? If states possessed concurrent power, did the contract clause impose any restrictions? Two weeks after the *Dartmouth College* decision Marshall spoke for an ostensibly unanimous Court in *Sturges*. Much of the opinion was characteristically dicta. Choosing not to distinguish between bankruptcy and insolvency, the chief justice allowed concurrent state power in the absence of congressional action. He then moved to the main question, impairment of the obligation of contract. Marshall found in the transaction between Sturges and Crowninshield every ingredient of a contract. Crowninshield had agreed to pay a specified sum at a specified time. "The law binds him to perform his undertaking, and this is, of course, the obligation of his contract," Marshall argued. Any law which relieved that obligation violated the contract clause. Because the retroactive features of the New York law did just that, Marshall found it clearly unconstitutional. The states could abolish imprisonment for debt, however, since such action discharged only the person of the debtor and left his obligation in full force.

Beneath the surface unanimity lay deep division. Todd did not participate because of illness. The remaining justices all compromised. Marshall opposed any state interference with contractual obligations, and he had the support of Story and Duval. But Washington accepted state insolvency laws that preceded the contract; and Livingston and Johnson favored the New York law. No doubt the justices shared some extended boardinghouse conferences, because the Court's opinion showed Johnson and Livingston surrendering on the question of the law's retroactive operation. The others, including Marshall, conceded a concurrent state power over bankruptcy.

The *Sturges* decision showed the lengths to which the brethren of the Marshall Court went in the interest of unanimity but contributed little to an effective settlement of debtor–

creditor relations. Compromise led to a general misunderstanding that the decision had prohibited all state bankruptcy legislation and alarmed both the business community and the mass of insolvent debtors. Yet Congress was unresponsive to pressure that it step into the void with another federal law.

That body was now burdened by old constitutional scruples. Repeated failures to adopt a nationwide system of internal improvements revealed renewed skepticism about implied powers and the old fear of centralized government. The heart of the matter was the relation between the states and the national government. Until the Marshall Court ruled on the scope of congressional power, the capacity of the eighteenth-century Constitution to meet the demands of national growth in the nineteenth century remained unclear. The opportunity for such a ruling came in *McCulloch* v. *Maryland*.

Delirious speculation in land and paper money, overexpansion of manufacturing, the dumping of British goods on the American market, and a precipitous drop in European prices for American produce were but some of the many stages on the road to depression in 1819. Most Americans, however, blamed their economic distress on a single, tempting target—the Second Bank of the United States.

The bank was open to criticism. The nationalistic Congress of 1816 had chartered it to bring order out of monetary chaos. In its first three years this economic colossus enraged the states by establishing branches within their borders without their consent, by competing with state banks in a reckless expansion of credit, and then by bringing a number of those state banks down with a sudden, drastic credit contraction. To make matters worse the branches were guilty of fraud, embezzlement, and general mismanagement. Resentment in the South and West was so intense that state after state imposed heavy taxes on the branches within their borders. By early 1819 public outcry against the "Monster" provoked an unsuccessful congressional effort to repeal the bank's charter.

Maryland's tax brought the "Bank Case" before the Marshall Court. James McCulloch, cashier of the Baltimore branch, refused to pay. The state sued in a widely recognized test case, and, after the bank lost twice in the state courts in 1818, *McCulloch* v. *Maryland* came before the Supreme Court. Few cases attracted such public interest. When the argument began on February 22, the courtroom was suffocatingly packed. Marshall dispensed with the Court's general rule permitting only two lawyers for each side. For nine days, six of the ablest lawyers in the nation argued every facet of the controversy. William Pinkney, Daniel Webster, and Attorney General William Wirt represented the bank; Joseph Hopkinson, Walter Jones, and Luther Martin argued for the state. Pinkney closed the argument with a dazzling three-day performance in his characteristic style—without notes but with plenty of attention to the ladies in the audience.

Four days later on March 17, Marshall delivered the Court's decision upholding the incorporation of the bank and striking down the state tax. The decision was unanimous, but the opinion was unmistakably his. Its ringing defense of implied power and its elaborate discussion of the relation between the nation and the states made it the outstanding statement of his judicial nationalism.

Marshall began with a refutation of the states' rights, strict construction argument. He could not allow the narrow view to shackle the nation's growth and to reduce the Constitution to a "splendid bauble." The Constitution was not a compact between sovereign states but an instrument of government created by the people "in their highest capacity" as sovereign individuals. Reason and the supremacy clause (Article VI) established that the national government, though limited to the enumerated powers, was supreme within its sphere of action. Any lawful act by the Congress took precedence over a state law.

The question remained whether incorporation of the bank, a power not among those enumerated, was a lawful act. A government could not be supreme unless it had broad discretion to choose the means by which to carry out its powers. Implied powers were not forbidden as they had been in the Articles of Confederation. The "necessary and proper" clause, which followed the enumeration of powers in Article I, section 8, gave Congress the power to pass "all laws which shall be necessary and proper for carrying into execution the foregoing powers." Our Constitution, he reminded his audience, was intended for "ages to come" and to be adaptable to the "various *crises* of human affairs." A narrow interpretation of "necessary" would render the nation unable to meet those "exigencies." So, his famous line ran, "Let the end be legitimate, let it be within the scope of the constitution, and all means which are appropriate, which are plainly adapted to that end, which are not prohibited, but consist with the letter and spirit of the constitution, are constitutional."

The chief justice conceded that in general taxation was a concurrent power. But, because "the power to tax involves the power to destroy," the question became one of national supremacy. The "unavoidable consequence of that supremacy" was that the states had no power, "by taxation or otherwise, to retard, impede, burden, or in any manner control, the operation of the constitutional laws enacted by congress to carry into execution the powers vested in the general government." Maryland's tax on the national bank notes was unconstitutional.

There was nothing surprising in this decision upholding the constitutionality of the bank. That question was so old that Pinkney had apologized during his argument for the endless repetition of that "threadbare" topic. The incorporation of the Second Bank of the United States in 1816 showed that even Republicans had abandoned their constitutional scruples on that issue. Even the protection against state taxation was not secure until a battle with Ohio produced another decision five years later.

The chief justice's explanation and his rationale for national supremacy and implied powers made the decision a constitutional landmark. Marshall knew that the Court's influence on the vital question of congressional power depended more on the persuasiveness of its reasoning than on the result in the immediate case. *McCulloch* was certainly persuasive. Its clarity, magisterial dignity, marching logic, memorable phrases, and air of righteous certainty made it seem unanswerable. The timing was also important. Just three weeks before the decision the heated congressional debate over slavery in Missouri joined the storm over *Sturges* to revive states' rights sentiments. *Niles' Weekly Register,* edited by Hezekiah Niles and the most widely read and influential newspaper in the country, blasted the opinion for its deadly blow at state sovereignty and gave *McCulloch* more publicity than any previous judicial decision.

Marshall expected a hostile reception, especially in Virginia, the fountainhead of states' rights and so recently a challenger of the Court's authority. He was not disappointed. Shortly after returning to Richmond in mid-March, he wrote Story, "Our opinion in the bank case has roused the sleeping spirit of Virginia if indeed it ever sleeps." The Virginia politicians had "no objection to a decision in favor of the bank," Marshall wrote Bushrod Washington, but "they required an obsequious, silent opinion without reason" and now pronounced the Court's "heretical reasoning . . . damnable." Marshall's principles, not the bank, rankled Virginians.

The opening salvo in Virginia's attack came when the *Enquirer* published two letters signed "Amphictyon" on March 30 and April 2. Written by William Brockenbrough, a Richmond judge and Junto member, the "Amphictyon" essays denounced Marshall's holding that national power emanated from the people, not the states, and that the "necessary and proper" clause should be broadly interpreted. Marshall was alarmed, because whatever the *Enquirer* published was always widely reprinted. Concerned lest the states' rights poison spread through the Union, he feared that "the constitution [would] be converted into the old confederation."

In June, Spencer Roane wrote a series of articles for the *Enquirer* using the name "Hampden." Predictably he set forth the strict constructionist view that the Union was only a league of sovereign states that had delegated specific powers to the national government. Roane's prestige was too great and the issue too serious for Marshall to let the matter pass in silence. He took up the pen and wrote nine essays in reply. They appeared in the *Gazette* in Alexandria, Virginia, under the pen name "A Friend of the Constitution."

These essays confirmed the depth of his commitment to nationalism. And his careful attention to the details of formal legal learning displayed a breadth of knowledge not usually attributed to the chief justice. Most important, the exhaustive—even tedious—explanation of *McCulloch* removed all doubt about Marshall's intentions on the subject of implied powers.

Roane's principal charge was that Marshall had given the Congress carte blanche. But Marshall denied that he had construed implied powers into a plenary grant to Congress to do whatever it pleased. *Marbury* stressed the limits to executive power but allowed the president discretion in the exercise of his political powers. *McCulloch* applied the same principle to Congress. Marshall never tired of repeating that the Court had not uttered a single syllable supporting an enlargement of congressional power by construction. On the contrary, the letter and spirit of the Constitution imposed judicially enforceable limits. In *McCulloch* he said clearly that the Court would not allow Congress to "adopt measures which are prohibited by the constitution" or to "pass laws for the accomplishment of objects not intrusted to the government."

Between 1819 and 1820, broader social and economic forces such as the Missouri debates over slavery kept the agitation alive. The Virginia legislature passed resolutions in February 1820 denouncing *McCulloch* and instructing Virginia's senators to push for a constitutional amendment creating a new tribunal to adjudicate federal–state problems. John Taylor's *Construction Construed and Constitutions Vindicated,* an able but rambling defense of states' rights, devoted five of its sixteen chapters to a refutation of *McCulloch.* Jefferson applauded

Taylor and chastised the Marshall Court as a "subtle corps of sappers and miners constantly working under ground to undermine the foundations of our confederated fabric."

Before the agitation subsided Virginia was forced to practice the states' rights principles she had been preaching. In 1821 two of her citizens haled her as a defendant before the Supreme Court of the United States. The case of *Cohens* v. *Virginia,* Marshall's effort to lay the axe to the hydra of states' rights, arose from trivia. The Cohen brothers had sold lottery tickets in Virginia under an act of Congress authorizing a lottery for Washington, D.C. Since Virginia law prohibited the sale of any but domestic tickets, the brothers were convicted in September 1820 in the Mayor's Court at Norfolk, fined one hundred dollars, and denied appeal to the state supreme court. Claiming a conflict between the Virginia and congressional laws, the brothers appealed directly to the Supreme Court on a writ of error. In accepting the appeal Marshall knew full well, as did Virginia, that this case presented questions of "great magnitude" concerning the nature of the Union and the Court's role as arbiter of the federal system.

The Old Dominion mustered all her resources for the coming battle. The governor alerted the legislature to the danger. That body condemned the pretensions of the national judiciary. Citing the Virginia and Kentucky resolutions, the Court of Appeals in the *Fairfax* case, state sovereignty, and the Eleventh Amendment, Virginia denied the Court's power to review the decisions of the state courts. Concerned solely with the jurisdictional question, Virginia instructed counsel to confine argument to that point.

On March 31, 1821, speaking for a unanimous Court, the chief justice hammered home the themes of *Martin* and *McCulloch.* In ratifying the Constitution, he said, the people had created an indivisible nation which necessarily subordinated the states to federal authority. One of the great duties of government was maintenance of the principles established in the Constitution, and the judiciary was "one of the instruments by which this duty may be peaceably performed." Marshall envisioned only chaos if each state were to be judge in constitutional questions arising within its borders. The Supreme Court's power of final decision was a necessary bulwark to an effective and binding national authority. Without it, the Constitution and Union would be prostrated "at the feet of every state in the Union." The Eleventh Amendment was intended only to protect states against suits by individuals and did not apply to an appeal from an action initiated by the state. Then, turning to the merits of the case, Marshall upheld the conviction of the Cohens on the ground that Congress had not intended to authorize lottery sales outside the District of Columbia. To this day, Marshall's *Cohens* opinion remains the basic precedent for national judicial supremacy.

If *McCulloch* had roused the sleeping spirits of Virginia, *Cohens* sent them into fits of rage. The case so angered Roane, who was sick and dying at Richmond, that he dashed off five more essays for the *Enquirer*, this time as "Algernon Sidney." He bitterly assailed judicial despotism for consolidating the national government on the ruins of the states and attacked Marshall as that "ultrafederal leader" who had hoodwinked his Republican brethren on the Court into uniting behind his extreme nationalism. James Madison declined to join the attack, believing that sound policy supported Marshall on appellate jurisdiction. Jefferson, now in his eighties, complained, however, that the Marshall Court was an "instrument which, working like gravity, without intermission, is to press us at last into one consolidated mass."

The acidity and virulence of Virginia's attack on the Court greatly distressed the chief justice. It was, he confided to Story, "a masked battery aimed at the government itself." The Court was the weakest governmental branch, "without patronage, & of course without power," and any diminution of its jurisdiction would be a "vital wound" to the Union. Story, like Marshall, feared the spread of heresy and the end of Union. "I trust in God," he wrote to the chief justice, "that the

Supreme Court will continue fearlessly to do its duty; & I pray that your invaluable life may be long preserved to guide us in our defense of the Constitution."

Marshall was particularly exasperated by Jefferson's part in the business. It was not difficult, he told Story, to pinpoint the reason for Jefferson's low opinion of the Court. The "great Lama of the mountains" was among the "most ambitious" and "most unforgiving" of men. His great power was over the mass of the people, and every check on the wild impulse of the moment was a check on his own power. Hence the hostility to an independent judiciary.

For his part, Jefferson continued to do all he could to slow the judicial engine of consolidation. Not the Court but Marshall troubled him. In *Cohens,* as in *Marbury,* the opposition won, as far as the outcome of the case, but the case offered Marshall the opportunity for instructional dicta and for precedents. Jefferson criticized precisely this quality of Marshall's decisions but could do nothing about it. He could do something about the troublesome unanimity in the opinions of 1819 to 1821. In 1822, suspicious about the true Republicanism of the majority, Jefferson took the extraordinary step of urging Johnson to have the individual justices speak their minds. The South Carolinian had long advocated separate opinions in constitutional cases; a year later he rebelled against Marshall.

The case of *Green* v. *Biddle* (1823) invalidated a Kentucky land law giving credit to occupants claimed by others in order to end the ceaseless conflict over titles of lands and provide some relief for settlers who were victims of lawyers and land speculators. The majority, speaking through Washington, ruled that the law violated a 1791 agreement between Kentucky and Virginia protecting the titles of the original claimants. In an extension of the contract clause, Washington held that this interstate agreement was a contract protected by the Constitution. Because of his long, intimate association with Kentucky lands, Marshall disqualified himself; Todd and Livingston were absent. Johnson wrote a concurring opinion whose stinging protest against the "hopeless imbecility" to which the majority's contract decisions reduced state governments made it a dissent in all but name.

Kentucky flatly refused to accept the decision. Squatters would not evacuate their lands, and state courts steadfastly upheld their claims. This clamor was a clear indication that the United States stood on the brink of profound and even revolutionary change. National expansion had, paradoxically, intensified sectional differences. The industrial revolution had taken hold of the Northeast; cotton increasingly tied the South to slavery; and six new western states brought the total to twenty-four in 1820. Debates on vital and sensitive issues —tariffs, internal improvements, bankruptcy, federal land policy, slavery—produced only shifting, episodic sectional alliances. No sense of national purpose and identity was apparent.

The Marshall Court was well-equipped to provide a blueprint for enduring growth. It had the advantage of continuous authority, which Congress lacked, and Marshall had built an institution which could speak with authority on important public issues, although only when cases came before it. Nonetheless, the unanimous decisions of 1819 to 1821 had addressed the deep social, economic, and political problems beneath the immediate cases. Marshall's searching discussions of the nature of the Union, of the scope of national power, and of the Court's role had the grand public purpose finely expressed by Story in 1815: "Let us extend the National authority over the whole extent of power given by the Constituition. . . . Let us prevent the possibility of a division, by creating great National interests which shall bind us in an indissoluble chain." Marshall wanted to demonstrate the Constitution's potential to meet the demands of a changing society.

The chief justice's constitutional analysis surely gave the flagging nationalists in Congress a new lease on life. The anti-Court criticism was a sign that the Court was doing its job. It also revealed that states' rights censures had as much to do with particular local interests as with a carefully thought out political theory. Virginia, the fountainhead of states' rights through 1821, warmly endorsed the *Green* decision, which favored Virginia land interests in Kentucky. Marshall's judicial nationalism was more attuned to the demands of national economic growth than the loud but disunified arguments of states' righters.

But the golden age of the Marshall Court had ended. Livingston's death in March 1823 produced the first breach in the Court's ranks since 1812, and Smith Thompson, who replaced him, frequently disagreed sharply with Marshall. Johnson had already indicated in *Green* that he would speak his own mind on constitutional questions. Both developments portended a retreat from the clarion nationalism of 1819 to 1821.

VIII

Retreat and Accommodation

1824–1831

"TIME," MARSHALL WROTE in 1821, "is marking on some of us more advances than we would be willing to acknowledge." A decade later that faint wistfulness had turned to despondent resignation and a brooding sense of failure. Time, it seemed to the seventy-six-year-old chief justice, was crumbling everything to which he had devoted his life.

In 1831 states' rights and belligerent talk of secession, especially in the South, more than ever threatened the Union. Economic growth and social and economic mobility had created widespread political unrest and a crusade against privilege. The movement toward universal manhood suffrage had already rewritten the constitutions of Massachusetts, New York, and Virginia, and the election of Andrew Jackson in 1828 had radically altered the presidency. Marshall became gloomy at the portents for government by what Story called "the wise and the good and the elevated in society."

The Court could extol the wisdom and necessity of Union, but it could not prevent the formation of states' rights factions. It could expound broad congressional powers, but it could not ensure their exercise. To make matters worse, the Court itself had changed. The number of dissenting and concurring opinions increased as four new justices complemented

Johnson's determination to bring division into the open. After 1830, when several of the recent appointees decided to abandon the communal living arrangements, the chief justice confided to Story that a "revolutionary spirit" was at work within the Court.

The Court accommodated the times. By making concessions to state power in commerce and contract cases, the Court retreated from the high nationalism and concern for property of 1819 to 1821. But the principles then established remained intact. The aging chief justice had built a better institution than he realized.

* * *

On August 7, 1807, the steamboat *Clermont* pulled away from the North River wharf in New York City for its maiden trip up the Hudson to Albany. Out of the commercial revolution that followed in its wake came the litigation leading to Marshall's classic statement of the commerce power of the national government in the "Steamboat Case" of *Gibbons* v. *Ogden* in 1824.

The New York legislature in 1808 granted a thirty-year monopoly on steam navigation in state waters to the steamer's builders, Robert R. Livingston and Robert Fulton, or their assignees. The two men envisioned a national network of steamboat lines, moving upstream and downstream, and able to carry more goods and passengers farther, faster, and cheaper than other forms of transport—all under their control. Accordingly, they petitioned state and territorial legislatures for monopolies like the one in New York. In April 1811 the Orleans Territorial legislature awarded them an eighteen-year monopoly on the lower Mississippi. By January 1812 one boat had completed an epic run down the Ohio and Mississippi to New Orleans. The age of steam navigation had begun. So had the reaction against special privilege.

Scores of speculating entrepreneurs, their appetites whetted by the commercial possibilities of steam navigation, challenged the Livingston–Fulton monopolies. In 1811 Albany businessmen launched a rival boat on the Albany–New York run. The monopolists fought back and won. In 1812 the highest state court upheld the monopoly on grounds that states had concurrent power with Congress to regulate commerce and that no conflict with a federal law existed. Livingston and Fulton were less successful in Louisiana, where they had to contend with unsympathetic courts, hostile public opinion, and, worse yet, superior competition. The dissatisfaction became epidemic. New Jersey, Connecticut, and Ohio prohibited Livingston–Fulton boats from their waterways, and several other states conferred their own monopolies. The steamboat seemed hopelessly snagged on states' rights, and the promise of free trade in an expanding national market seemed about to dissolve in commercial civil war.

The monopoly's efforts to quash the New Jersey competition gave rise to *Gibbons* v. *Ogden*. Aaron Ogden, former New Jersey governor, tried for several years to defy the monopoly by operating a steam ferry from Elizabethtown to New York City. By 1815, however, he gave in and purchased a license from the Livingston assignees (both Livingston and Fulton were dead). Then he acquired a truculent partner in Thomas Gibbons. The testy partnership broke apart in 1818 when Gibbons, aided by the talented but unscrupulous young Cornelius Vanderbilt, started his own ferry. When the competition began quickly to eat into Ogden's profits, he took Gibbons into court. The New York court granted a permanent injunction against Gibbons in 1820. Gibbons appealed to the United States Supreme Court, claiming that the New York monopoly under which Ogden was operating conflicted with the Federal Coasting Act of 1793, under which he held a license, and with the commerce clause of the Constitution (Article I, section 8). Numerous delays occurred for technical reasons. Finally, in 1824, the Court got its opportunity to clarify the meaning of the commerce clause.

Nationalists and states' rights advocates were at odds over internal improvements. Presidents Madison and Monroe had vetoed bills on the grounds that the commerce clause did not authorize a positive federal program of internal improvements. While the Court considered *Gibbons,* Congress debated a bill to provide a federal survey of road and canal routes. The implications troubled John Randolph, who warned that if Congress possessed broad power over commerce, "they may *emancipate every slave in the United States.*" Increasingly aware of its minority status in the Union, the South also opposed the commerce power in debates on the Tariff of 1824.

Marshall was aware of this political climate, and the throng of congressmen, reporters, and Washington ladies spilling into the aisles of the basement chambers reminded him this was no ordinary case. Both sides had retained eminent counsel. Suing for Gibbons were Daniel Webster and Attorney General William Wirt; defending Ogden were Thomas J. Oakley, New York attorney general, and Thomas Addis Emmet, the brilliant Irish expatriate and veteran Livingston–Fulton attorney. For five days these giants examined every aspect of the controversy. Webster and Wirt emphasized exclusive national power over commerce. Oakley and Emmet justified concurrent state power in the absence of a conflict between state and national law, which they did not see in this case.

On March 2, 1824, Marshall read his opinion striking down the New York monopoly. He began by expounding the Constitution—in this case the clause that gave Congress the power "to regulate commerce with foreign nations, and among the several states, and with the Indian tribes." Strict construction of this and other enumerated powers would cripple the national government. The meaning of those powers was intimately connected to the purpose for which they were conferred; and freedom of commerce among the states was a primary purpose of the Constitution, prerequisite to Union and to national economic growth.

It remained to apply this broad, nationalist interpretation to the words "regulate," "commerce," and "among the several states." Commerce, Marshall proclaimed, embraced traffic, navigation, and "every species of commercial intercourse." The power to regulate was the power "to prescribe the rule by which commerce is to be governed" and had no limits other than those "prescribed in the constitution." Commerce which was "among the states" could not stop at the external boundary of each state but might be introduced into the interior. Congress, in short, could regulate commerce wherever it existed.

Just such a sweeping definition of the national commerce power had alarmed Randolph and the states' rights defenders in the congressional debates over internal improvements. Hence, though his nationalism strongly intimated exclusive national power, the chief justice was reluctant to declare it. Sensitive to the practical difficulties of the federal system, he groped his way to a formula that would accommodate state regulation of local problems and the demands of free trade for an expanding national economy. National power, he said, did not extend to those concerns "which are completely within a particular state, which do not affect other states, and with which it is not necessary to interfere for the purpose of executing some of the general powers of the government."

Marshall was announcing a doctrine of selective exclusiveness. States could enact inspection, health, and pilotage laws which might affect interstate commerce, but the chief justice would not admit this enactment as an exercise of a concurrent commerce power. He preferred to call it the state police power. Congress could enter this area, too, if the national interest required it. By implication, the Court would have the responsibility of deciding the extent of permissible state activity in the future on a case by case basis.

Marshall found a way to resolve the "Steamboat" controversy in Gibbons's claim of a conflict between the 1793 Federal

Coasting Act and the New York laws. The 1793 law required only the licensing of vessels engaged in the coastal trade. But, by stretching its meaning, Marshall turned it into an implicit guarantee of free navigation on the waterways of the United States. Because the New York laws impeded free navigation, they conflicted with this national law and were, therefore, void.

Once more Marshall had used a case to expound the meaning of the Constitution. This course was "unavoidable," he explained, because "powerful and ingenious minds" used strict construction to "explain away the constitution of our country, and leave it a magnificent structure indeed, to look at, but totally unfit to use."

With the exception of Smith Thompson—who was absent due to his daughter's death—the decision was unanimous. Johnson, by now completely determined to state his own opinion in constitutional cases, wrote a powerful concurring opinion asserting what Marshall had not—that congressional power over commerce "must be exclusive" and that the grant of this power carried with it "the whole subject, leaving nothing for the state to act upon."

Gibbons was as widely acclaimed as Marshall's earlier nationalist decisions had been condemned. Most of the country saw only the demise of a hated and obnoxious monopoly. Newspapers in New York and across the land reprinted the full opinion. This "masterpiece of judicial reasoning concerns every citizen," ran a typical comment, because "unlimited scope is now afforded to enterprise and capital in steam navigation." For once, a Marshall decision had articulated popular aspirations. His comprehensive definition of the national commerce power had made it possible for Congress to act, although social, economic, political, and sectional pressures prevented it from doing so.

The explosive issue of slavery was partly responsible for Johnson's vigorous concurrence in *Gibbons*. In June 1822 Charleston, South Carolina, had learned of a planned slave uprising led by the free black Denmark Vesey. After brutally suppressing the revolt, South Carolina enacted a law reflecting its belief that free black sailors on ships in Charleston harbor had incited the unrest and requiring that all such sailors be jailed until their ships departed.

Charleston was Johnson's home. A strong libertarian, he had publicly attacked the high-handed and summary trial and execution of the conspirators. Then Henry Elkison, a black sailor and British subject, petitioned Johnson's circuit court for a writ of habeas corpus. In *Elkison* v. *Deliesseline* (1823), Johnson boldly held the law unconstitutional, because it violated a treaty with Great Britain and the "paramount and exclusive" power of Congress to regulate foreign commerce. Johnson ruled that the grant to Congress swept "away the whole subject" and left "nothing for the states to act upon." Otherwise, the Union would become like the old Confederation—a "mere rope of sand." A wave of indignation swept the South. South Carolina defied the decision. More ominously, there was free talk of secession and forcible resistance.

Marshall thought Johnson's opinion had unnecessarily fueled the fire at which states' rights extremists "roast the Judicial Department." The chief justice was more circumspect. In a similar case on his circuit in 1820 he had disposed of the commerce question more prudently to avoid being snagged "in a hedge composed entirely of thorny State-Rights." Because it was not "absolutely necessary" to consider the constitutional question, Marshall, unlike Johnson, "escaped on the construction of the act." He was "not fond of butting against a wall in sport." *Gibbons* showed Marshall's penchant for avoiding the practical difficulties of constitutional questions and for "escaping" by construction.

Before the decade was over he had to deal with the questions left unanswered in 1824. On the problem of slavery the chief justice mirrored the painful ambivalence of his times. The "peculiar institution" had always been a part of his environment. He had acquired his first slave, a servant named

Robin, as a wedding present from his father in 1783 and owned others until his death in 1835. His will emancipated Robin, but in the carefully guarded fashion of the day. Old Robin should be freed "if he *chuses* to conform to the laws on that subject," and Virginia law required free blacks to leave the state. If he chose to go to Liberia, Marshall awarded him one hundred dollars; if not, fifty dollars—hardly a magnanimous reward for more than a half century of service. But, and this point was the decisive one, if it were "impracticable to liberate" Robin, the old man could select his master from among Marshall's children and should be treated always as a "faithful and meritorious servant." Throughout his life, then, Marshall never violated the code of the Virginia gentry.

He did not consider slavery good and, like Jefferson and Monroe, was troubled by the evil of it. Slavery, after all, deprived men of the natural right to enjoy the fruits of their labors; and Marshall regarded slaves as human beings. But they were also property. Therein lay his dilemma. State law and the Constitution sanctioned the institution, and Marshall's passionate commitment to Union and to the protection of property constrained him to proclaim slavery legitimate—even expedient in the short run. Although he looked forward to the day when the evil would be purged from the land, the social, economic, and political costs of emancipation made it unlikely without "convulsion."

Slavery became a problem for John Marshall when it threatened the Union and social stability after 1820. The Southern states "seemed to cherish the evil & to view with immovable prejudice & dislike every thing which may tend to diminish it. I do not wonder that they should resist any attempt . . . to interfere with the rights of property, but they have a feverish jealousy of measures which may do good without the hazard of harm that is, I think, very unwise."

As a nationalist Marshall worried about both the strident states' rights defense of slavery and the abolitionist attacks on the Constitution. But he also worried that the "slave population" itself threatened "calamity & mischief." Fear of slave insurrection and race war had pervaded Virginia since the abortive Gabriel uprising against Richmond in 1800, intensified after the Vesey affair, and turned to hysteria after the Nat Turner or Southampton insurrection in 1831, the bloodiest slave revolt in American history.

At the Virginia Convention of 1832—called to consider the emergency produced by the Turner insurrection—Marshall's son Thomas echoed his father's sentiments. He objected to slavery, because "it is ruinous to the whites—retards improvement—roots out an industrious population—banishes the yeoman of the country—deprives the spinner, the weaver, the smith, the shoemaker, the carpenter, of employment and support." As Virginia was "inundated by one black wave," she suffered the "curse of a wasteful, idle, reckless population."

Marshall found a palliative in the American Colonization Society, organized in 1816, with the prime purpose of the removal of troublesome free blacks by colonizing them in Africa (Liberia was established through its efforts). Even slaveholders supported it for that reason; Bushrod Washington, its first president, was a good example. It offered no hope to slaves. In short, it sought to preserve the Union and property in slaves and stood against insurrection and for white supremacy. Marshall was president of the Richmond auxiliary from 1823 until his death. "The removal of our colored population is," he wrote in 1831, "a common object, by no means confined to the slave states. . . . The whole Union would be strengthened by it, and relieved from a danger, whose extent can scarcely be estimated."

Slavery posed the same dilemma for the Marshall Court as it did for Marshall. Because the Constitution sanctioned slavery, and slaves were legally property, the justices were restrained from challenging the institution. The Court could not declare the Constitution unconstitutional. And an institutional restraint complicated matters: The Court could act only in *cases*. The slavery questions that came before the

Marshall Court involved settled points of state or international law and did not present the opportunity to rule either on the legality or the constitutionality of slavery—whatever the justices' convictions on its morality.

Concern for the Constitution, property, judicial propriety, and the rule of law produced poignant moments, as in *The Antelope* of 1825. This case raised the question of the legality of the slave trade under international law. An American warship had captured a vessel carrying nearly three hundred Africans destined for sale into slavery. Because the Africans had earlier been taken from Portuguese and Spanish slave ships, officials of those countries petitioned the Court to return their property. Marshall's opinion noted that the case brought the "sacred rights of liberty and property" into conflict, but that "this Court must not yield to feelings which might seduce it from the path of duty, but must obey the mandates of the law." He thought the slave trade an "abhorrent" contradiction of the natural law. Nonetheless international law sanctioned the trade and required the return of the property to its owners. The decision was unanimous. The Court could not act on slavery. But neither could it isolate itself from this spreading infection in the body politic.

The years after 1826 saw marked changes in the Marshall Court. Rapid commercial development dramatically increased its work load, and docket congestion became a problem. During the 1825 term the Court disposed of only 38 of 165 cases on its docket, and it fell further behind with each passing year. The growth of the docket increased the circuit duties of the justices, and Congress offered them no relief. Instead, in 1826 it lengthened the Court's term and added to the justices' problems.

Marshall fretted also over the new independent spirit within the Court. Three new members between 1826 and 1830 did nothing to retard it. Todd died in 1826—some charged that Congress had murdered him by forcing him to ride 3360 miles on circuit each year. His replacement was Robert Trimble, an able Kentucky lawyer and federal judge. But Trimble died in 1828, and John McLean, former judge of the Ohio supreme court and postmaster-general under Monroe and John Quincy Adams, came to the Bench. Then, in 1830, Bushrod Washington died. His place was filled by Henry Baldwin of Pennsylvania. None of the new justices were as interested in unanimity as their predecessors had been. The number of separate opinions therefore increased as dramatically as the docket. Marshall still continued to do more work than his brethren, but he was no longer able—or, in one case, willing—to strike the old consensus.

The new tone appeared strikingly with the first case of the 1827 term. *Ogden* v. *Saunders* involved the issue that *Sturges* had largely skirted—the respective powers of Congress and the states over bankruptcy. Revealing the tension within the Court, the majority spoke seriatim and against Marshall. Johnson ruled that congressional power over bankruptcy was not exclusive and that, in the absence of congressional legislation, state acts which applied only to contracts made after their passage were constitutional. Thompson, Trimble, and even Washington also upheld the state act. Marshall, joined by Story and Duval, stuck to his *Sturges* opinion and wrote his only dissent in a constitutional case. He argued the majority's ruling rendered the contract clause "inanimate, inoperative, and unmeaning" and, by destroying the confidence of the "good and the wise," endangered the nation's prosperity.

Three years later Marshall himself modified the *Dartmouth College* decision. In *Providence Bank* v. *Billings* (1830) he upheld a Rhode Island law taxing banks. The taxing power was vital to government, and all individuals, including corporate individuals, should share public burdens. Unless the bank's charter contained an "express contract" not to tax, no exemption could be implied.

In 1827 and again in 1829, when Marshall dealt with the question of state and national power over commerce he had left open in *Gibbons*, he tried to adjust the Court's policy to the times. At issue in *Brown* v. *Maryland* was a state law requiring importers to purchase a fifty-dollar license. Brown and Company, a prominent Baltimore firm, convicted of importing and selling dry goods without that license, appealed on the grounds that the state law violated the constitutional provision prohibiting the states from taxing imports (Article I, section 10) and the national power to regulate foreign commerce. The chief justice ruled the Maryland law unconstitutional. He asserted that by taxing the right to sell imports, the state had taxed the imports. At what point did national control over imports give way to an admitted concurrent state power to tax? That question was difficult, but Marshall nonetheless attempted a formula: When the importer incorporated and mixed up the thing imported with the mass of property in the country, it lost its distinctive character as an import and became subject to the taxing power of the state; but while remaining the importer's property, in his warehouse, in its original form or package, a tax was plainly an unconstitutional duty on imports. But Marshall would not go further to assert an exclusive national power to regulate foreign commerce. Once more he avoided a black-and-white distinction between state and national power. As in *Gibbons*, the chief justice conceded the state power to protect public health and safety by controlling dangerous articles like gunpowder or ordering the destruction of "infectious or unsound" imports. But, he emphasized, such actions were part of the police power, not regulations of imports or commerce.

Brown settled nothing beyond the immediate case. The question of state and national power over commerce remained and came before the Court again two years later.

Willson v. *Blackbird Creek Marsh Co.* (1829) was Marshall's last commerce case. Under authority of a Delaware law, the Blackbird Creek Marsh Company had built a dam across the navigable tidal creek. A vessel owned by a man named Willson broke down the dam trying to get around the obstruction. The company sued for damages and won in state court. Willson appealed to the Supreme Court, claiming a right to navigate under the same federal coasting law which had supported Gibbons against New York.

This time Marshall upheld the state law for a unanimous Court. Ironically, as Willson's lawyers had argued, *Gibbons* should have controlled the case. The same federal coasting law was available to invalidate the state law. Marshall, however, ignored the federal law and ruled the Delaware law a proper exercise of the powers reserved to the states. Delaware's effort to improve property values along the creek banks and to protect public health by draining the marsh waters did not conflict with the dormant power of Congress to regulate commerce.

Gibbons, Brown, and *Willson* revealed Marshall's pragmatism. Accommodating to the political and economic pressures of the times, Marshall had both enlarged national power and left the states a measure of control over local affairs. His circumspect opinions reserved to the Court the power to make policy choices on future state legislation by pragmatically judging the circumstances of each case in relation to national needs.

To the chief justice—now in his seventies—the times were ominous. "I begin to fear," he lamented to Story in 1827, "that our constitution is not to be so long lived as its real friends have hoped. . . . I shall not live to see and bewail the consequences of these furious passions which are breaking loose upon us."

The Union was afflicted with a terminal disease. Andrew Jackson's fervid drive for the presidency in 1828 plunged Marshall into gloom. He feared the appeal to the "sovereign will of the people" and the portrayal of the contest as one between aristocracy and democracy. He deplored the way the battle intruded into congressional affairs, and he abhorred the savage character assassination of the campaign. Such pandering to an aroused and passionately partisan people was not what Marshall had had in mind in 1788 when he spoke of a "well-regulated democracy."

The raucous campaign enveloped the chief justice. The other Supreme Court justices were actively involved. Story and Washington were openly in support of President John Quincy Adams, and Thompson ran for governor of New York to carry that state for Adams. Johnson declared for Adams. Then, in the spring of 1828, a Jacksonian newspaper, the *Marylander,* reported that Marshall said it was his "solemn duty" to vote in this election, "for should Jackson be elected, I shall look upon the government as virtually dissolved." Stung at seeing his private remarks emblazoned on front pages across the country, Marshall printed a denial of the words but not the spirit of the remark. He did not object to anyone knowing that he favored Adams, but he did object "to being represented in the character of a furious partisan. Intemperate language does not become my age or office, and is foreign to my disposition and habits." He was vexed at the impression that he would use "language which could be uttered only by an angry party man."

The more he pondered the implications of Jackson's victory, the more pessimistic Marshall became. "The present mode of electing the president," he reluctantly concluded, roused the "worst of passions" and embittered the "vast masses" against each other. "Scarcely is a President elected before the machinations, respecting a successor, commence. . . . All those who are in office, all those who want office, are put in motion." Seeing nothing but discouraging prospects, the chief justice favored some "less turbulent, and less dangerous" method of selecting the president—even a plan to pick one by lot from among the members of the Senate.

Marshall had watched the pressure for equal representation and the elimination of property restrictions rewrite the Massachusetts and New York constitutions between 1820 and 1821. Then, on the day he presided over Jackson's inauguration, he learned that Richmond wanted him to become a delegate to the Virginia Convention of 1829—called, he knew, for the same purpose.

Criticism of the old state constitution of 1776 had begun to swell after the War of 1812, centered mostly on the issue of representation. Virginians of the rapidly growing and larger but less numerous western counties complained of disproportionate political power in the Tidewater. Westerners pressed for representation based on the white population and for universal white manhood suffrage. They had fought for a constitutional convention to produce these changes for over a decade and finally succeeded in 1828.

Marshall initially declined to stand for election as a delegate. He felt that he lacked the physical powers to represent his constituents' interests effectively. Predictably, the citizens of Richmond elected him anyway. "I am ashamed of my weakness and irresolution," he told Story. "I have acted like a girl addressed by a gentleman she does not positively dislike, but is unwilling to marry. She is sure to yield to the advice and persuasion of her friends."

John Marshall joined the other delegates when the convention met in the House of Delegates in October 1829. This was the last gathering of Virginia's Revolutionary statesmen. Among the distinguished delegates Marshall saw old friends and old enemies whose lives embraced the history of Virginia and the nation since 1776—James Madison, now a feeble seventy-nine; James Monroe, who would be dead within a year; William Branch Giles; and John Randolph. Placing their differences behind them, these old men came to defend the old order against challengers. In such company and for more than three months Marshall argued for a "well-regulated democracy," the property restriction on voting, and the independence of the state judiciary. But age had taken its toll. He spoke briefly and infrequently, although he still captured attention by the force of his reasoning.

In the debate on representation Marshall played only a small part, but he helped vote a crushing defeat for the democratic reformers. The fight to eliminate property qualifications on voting led to a compromise which slightly extended

the franchise but still preserved a "substantial property qual-
ification." In discussions of the judiciary, he defended the
justices of the peace as the "best men" in counties, the "peacemakers" and guarantors of "complete internal quiet"; his arguments against tampering with a proven system prevailed.
Marshall also passionately defended the independence of the
judiciary, the cause to which he had devoted the preceding
twenty-eight years. It was vital, he said, that the judge be
"perfectly and completely independent, with nothing to influence or control him but God and his conscience." His eloquent summation drove home the depth of his conviction
on this subject. "The greatest scourge an angry Heaven ever
inflicted upon an ungrateful and a sinning people, was an
ignorant, a corrupt, or a dependent Judiciary. Will you draw
down this curse upon Virginia?" The convention answered by
voting a resounding "No!"

Marshall had no time to savor his successful defense of the
Virginia judiciary. Arriving at Washington for the Court's
1830 term, he found the Senate embroiled in a great debate
over the nature of the Union, states' rights, and, most de-
pressing of all, the power and jurisdiction of the Court. In
the course of this debate Robert Y. Hayne of South Carolina
advanced the doctrine of nullification, arguing that a state has
a right to declare national laws unconstitutional. Daniel Webster answered Hayne with an eloquent defense of "Liberty and
Union, now and forever, one and inseparable." The Constitution and Section 25 of the 1789 Judiciary Act, he concluded,
clearly established the Court as the ultimate arbiter of all
constitutional questions.

In the midst of this argument the Court invalidated a state
law. *Craig* v. *Missouri* grew out of an attempt to ease financial
distress. The legislature had enacted a law establishing loan
offices where Missourians could purchase certificates by sign-
ing promissory notes. These certificates became "money" in
Missouri. Hiram Craig had given a promissory note but then
later refused to pay. The state sued him and won in state

court. Craig then appealed to the Supreme Court on a writ of error, charging that the Missouri law violated the constitutional provision (Article I, section 10) prohibiting states from issuing bills of credit. Thomas Hart Benton, an ardent Jacksonian senator from Missouri, defended the state with a truculent attack on the Court's power to summon a sovereign state to appear. Marshall's opinion not only invalidated the law as unconstitutional but also addressed the criticisms of Benton and his states' rights Senate colleagues. To the warning against offending the dignity of a sovereign state, his answer was straightforward and uncompromising: "This department can listen only to the mandates of law, and can tread only that path which is marked out by duty." Johnson, McLean, and Thompson dissented in favor of state power. The lack of unanimity at a time when the Court was under attack upset Marshall.

As he worried about the "revolutionary spirit" on the Court and the general state of the nation in the spring of 1831, Marshall's health failed. While on circuit in North Carolina he suffered excruciating pain when making sudden movements or urinating. Throughout the summer he tried home remedies, "none of which were of any service to me, but which had a sensible influence on my general health. My nerves, my digestion, and my head were seriously affected." Unable to concentrate, he determined to resign at the close of the year. In his confused state he had miscalculated the presidential election for the fall of 1831 and had decided that a defeat of Jackson would relieve his anxiety about a successor. By September he could no longer stand the pain and went to Philadelphia to consult with the foremost surgeon in America, Dr. Philip Syng Physick, who diagnosed the ailment as bladder stones and recommended surgical removal. Marshall agreed. On October 13, he underwent surgery, eager, he said, to be cured or to end his suffering through death. The operation, an astonishing success, removed roughly one thousand stones. Marshall recovered quickly.

Within a month he was able to get out of bed, totter across the room, and use a pen. On November 10, he wrote Story of his plan to take the steamboat to Richmond the following week in time to open his circuit court on November 22. Still, he complained of the "disagreeable necessity of taking medicine continually to prevent new formations" and of submitting to "a severe and most unsociable regimen. Such are the privations of age."

The sorest privation was yet to come. Polly fell gravely ill. By mid-December she was confined to her bed. "My fears are stronger than my hopes," Marshall confided to his brother James. Polly sank rapidly, Marshall constantly at her side. He was there on Christmas Eve when she placed the locket containing the snippet of hair around his neck. And he was there on Christmas Day when she died.

Marshall simply could not accommodate the shock of Polly's death. But he mourned in private and several weeks later presided once more at Court. At the boardinghouse, however, Story once found him in tears, and the chief justice told his close friend that he rarely passed a night without weeping over his wife. Christmas 1832—"this day of joy & festivity to the whole Christian world"—for the chief justice was "the anniversary of the keenest affliction which humanity can sustain. . . . It was the will of Heaven to take to itself the companion who had sweetened the choicest part" of his life, who "had rendered toil a pleasure," had partaken of all his feelings, "& was enthroned in the inmost recesses" of his heart. "Never," he wrote, "can I cease to feel the loss & to deplore it. . . . I have lost her! And with her I have lost the solace of my life!" Yet she remained the companion of his retired hours. When he was alone and unoccupied, his mind unceasingly turned to her.

IX

"Dragging On"

1831–1835

THE STEADY DETERIORATION of the Court and the Union after 1831 did nothing to lift the pall that Polly's death had cast over John Marshall. Old colleagues, institutions, and principles vanished at every turn. The Court was only a pale reflection of the institution Marshall had built into the arbiter of the Constitution. Illness and vacancies now aggravated the old problems of the docket and the "revolutionary spirit" of division. On important constitutional questions postponement rather than decision became the rule. Jackson's victorious war against the Bank of the United States and the Indian removal policy revealed the leveling, intolerant democracy Marshall feared. And states' rights fearlessly challenged national authority as Georgia's defiance on the Cherokee question and South Carolina's 1832 nullification of the tariffs of 1828 and 1832 demonstrated. Convinced that the world had gone *topsy turvy*, the aging chief justice sank into gloom. "What is to become of us and of our constitution?" became the haunting question of his last years.

*   *   *

Marshall demonstrated his green old age in 1832. *Worcester* v. *Georgia* was the last effort of the Georgia Cherokees to halt state encroachment on their lands. In a bold but calculated decision, the chief justice invalidated Georgia's Indian law. The decision had no practical effect; by 1838 the Cherokees, forcibly removed from their lands, set forth on "The Trail of Tears" to territory west of the Mississippi. The Court's handling of the Cherokee cases from 1830 to 1832, however, revealed a Marshall still ready to do battle when he could limit the risks by carefully choosing the battleground. The Cherokees served him well.

The Cherokee cases arose from the struggle over land—the Indians had it; the states claimed it. The national government's solution was an ambiguous blend of token humanitarianism and ruthlessness; the effect was a series of hopelessly contradictory obligations. The United States treated the Indians as sovereign nations and made treaties, such as that with the Cherokees in 1791, purchasing lands the Indians wished to sell and guaranteeing those they wished to retain. The official presumption underlying these treaties—that the Indians wished to sell—masked the bribery, cajolery, fraud, and outright intimidation which usually forced them into wishing. The result was the steady removal of Indians from their ancestral lands and an expectation of more sales as the need arose. Acting on this expectation, the government promised to remove the Indians from the states. In Georgia's 1802 Yazoo cession, for example, the United States pledged to extinguish by peaceful and reasonable means all remaining Indian titles to Georgia lands. The national government had promised the Indians to protect their lands and had promised Georgia to remove the Indians from those same lands.

The inevitable crunch came in the 1820s when the Georgia Cherokees had become civilized. With the aid and encouragement of the federal government they had taken up farming, they owned plantations and slaves, and they had developed schools and a written language. They had grown attached to their lands and decided to sell no more. Impatient at the reluctance of the government to fulfill its 1802 agreement, Georgia in 1824 took matters into its own hands, asserted jurisdiction over all lands within its boundaries, and denied the authority of the United States to bind its hands by treaties with the Indians.

Georgia's intransigence exposed the bankruptcy of national policy. The Creeks in western Georgia first felt the effects. President John Quincy Adams had threatened to use force to protect the Creeks; Georgia had threatened force to defend her interests. The ominous rattling of sabres ceased when the Creeks voluntarily ceded their lands and moved West. Impressed by the fate of the Creeks, the Cherokees called a convention in 1827, declared their independence of state authority, and drafted a constitution. Georgia retaliated in 1828 and 1829 with a series of repressive laws dividing up Cherokee lands and nullifying their constitution and laws. The Cherokees, in turn, petitioned Washington to protect their rights under the treaty of 1791.

Cherokee determination forced Jackson to resolve the ambiguity of Indian policy. In the spring of 1829 he denied the right of the Cherokees to set up an independent nation within Georgia and informed them that he had no authority to meddle in the internal affairs of a state. In December he asked Congress to establish an Indian territory west of the Mississippi and outside the boundaries of any state. Those Indians who wanted to preserve their identity and culture could move to this new territory. Others could stay and submit to Georgia law. After a lengthy debate through the spring of 1830, Congress passed the Indian Removal Bill.

Jackson and the Congress had only declared what had been policy all along. The rhetoric of opposition to removal was more anti-Jackson than pro-Indian. The president did not have much choice. Neither states' rights sentiment nor the democratic press for equality would tolerate Indian nations inside state borders or Indian exemption from state law. In the politically explosive climate of 1830 removal seemed a practical and humane way to protect the Indians.

Marshall slipped into this unfolding tragedy. As with slavery, practical humanitarianism governed his attitudes. He believed that "the principles of humanity and justice" should govern American conduct toward the "aborigines," when the country could pursue them without exposing itself to "the most afflicting calamities." On the other hand, the chief justice never doubted the superiority of white over Indian civilization, and he recognized the demands of expansion.

That the "red man" was a "fierce and dangerous enemy" in the seventeenth and eighteenth centuries justified "every endeavor to remove [him] to a distance from civilized settlements." By the late 1820s, however, Marshall viewed the Indians as a "helpless people depending on our magnanimity and justice for the preservation of their existence." Indignant at the government's abandonment of the Creeks, he told Story in 1828 that each oppression impressed "a deep stain on the American character." He followed the 1830 debates on removal with "profound attention" and lamented that both president and Congress had not shown more strength. But beneath this humanitarian veneer lay a deeper concern for the integrity of the government of the United States. Georgia's defiant disregard of treaties with the Indians not only raised the specter of disunion but also brought into question the honor of the United States. Jackson and the Congress should have been less eager to accede.

Within three days after enactment of the Removal Bill, the anti-Jackson forces, loudest in opposition to removal, began laying plans to capture the presidency in 1832. Webster and others who hoped to use the Court as a forum for discrediting Jackson urged the Cherokees to hire eminent counsel to test their rights. They hoped that the Court would uphold the Indians and embarrass the president.

After thirty years of struggling to keep the Court aloof from the rough-and-tumble world of partisan politics, Marshall now faced one of his severest tests. Partisan maneuvers placed the Court on a collision course with Georgia and Jackson.

Trouble began almost immediately. The Cherokees retained William Wirt, who thought that as a foreign nation they should appeal directly to the original jurisdiction of the Supreme Court for an injunction to restrain Georgia. To resolve doubts about the wisdom of this course, he took the unusual step of asking a close friend, Virginia Judge Dabney Carr, to solicit Marshall's advice. Although Marshall refrained from giving advice, he did not discourage the effort to get a Supreme Court decision.

Meanwhile, an unplanned case revealed the awful dimensions of the Court's problem. A Cherokee named Corn Tassels murdered another tribesman within Indian territory. Arrested and tried before a Georgia court, Tassels pleaded that the treaty between the United States and the Cherokees provided for trial only by his own nation. The court rejected this defense, found him guilty, and sentenced him to be hanged. Wirt applied to the Supreme Court for a writ of error, which Marshall granted. Georgia stood on its sovereignty and refused to appear. The governor and the legislature publicly denounced this latest example of judicial usurpation and threatened to block enforcement with arms if necessary. Then, to demonstrate its contempt, Georgia executed Corn Tassels.

As 1831 opened the issue was no longer the Cherokees but the authority of the Supreme Court. Despite the rulings in *Martin* and *Cohens,* that old sore kept opening. "The affair of Georgia, so far as Tassels is concerned," Story wrote a friend, "has probably passed by with his death. But we are threatened with the general question in another form." Wirt entered the case of *Cherokee Nation* v. *Georgia* on the Court's docket for the 1831 term. Story preferred not to touch the question "at this moment" but told his friend that judges were not free "to choose times and occasions. We must do our duty as we may." Marshall shared those sentiments.

Georgia did not appear when the argument opened on March 5. Wirt gave one of the most eloquent performances of his career, defending the Cherokees' right to sue as a foreign nation and the Court's authority to issue the injunction. Then, in a bold challenge to Jackson, he asserted the president's duty to enforce Court orders, hinting at impeachment if he failed to do so.

On the last day of the term Marshall dismissed the case for want of jurisdiction. History, precedent, and international law, he said, would not allow the Court to consider the Cherokees "foreign nations" within the meaning of the Constitution. But that did not mean they were totally dependent upon the states. Looking to the peculiar relations between the national government and the Indians, Marshall labeled the Cherokees "domestic dependent nations." They were wards of the United States. But if wrongs had been inflicted, the Court was not the tribunal to redress the past. Other questions, such as property rights, the Court could handle "in a proper case with the proper parties." By denying jurisdiction, Marshall prevented a clash with Georgia or Jackson, but he also hinted that the Court sympathized with the merits of the Cherokees' case and pointed the way to new litigation.

Rumors now circulated that the disheartened Cherokees were willing to agree to removal. Georgia and the Jacksonians were elated. The Court's opinion seemed to vindicate Georgia's stand against the Indians and the president's refusal to interfere. But the Cherokee litigation, with all its moral, constitutional, and political implications, was not over.

Marshall was not happy with the result. He would have preferred a decision upholding the principles of "humanity and justice" and putting Georgia in her place. The form of the case had left him no choice within the law. But he had left an opening and moved to exploit it in the spring of 1831.

He encouraged Story and Thompson to write opinions explaining their dissent after the Court had risen. This unusual step revealed Marshall's eagerness for a correct decision, and Thompson's dissenting opinion went into great detail suggesting the manner in which another case might come before the Court.

Marshall also encouraged an appeal to public opinion. The Court reporter, Richard Peters, decided to publish a full account of the case for public consumption. This report—including arguments of counsel, a legal opinion by Chancellor Kent favoring the Cherokees, and relevant laws and treaties in addition to the justices' opinions—was heavily weighted in favor of the Indians. Marshall was "glad to see the whole case" brought to public attention. In a letter to Peters, the chief justice explained that he had written a narrow opinion in *Cherokee Nation* because he "did not think it truly proper to pass the narrow limits that circumscribed the matter on which the decision of the court turned." The dissenting opinions fully covered the other side of the question.

These maneuvers helped bring the *Worcester* case before the Court. This time the issue was a conflict between state and national law. Although the Cherokees were very much involved, the plaintiff was a white American who had defied Georgia law to bring the matter before the Court. A more "proper case" could not have been arranged.

After the execution of Corn Tassels in December 1830, Georgia passed a law forbidding whites to enter Indian territory without a license. Samuel A. Worcester, a Vermont missionary who had been working with the Cherokees for years as postmaster at their capital of New Echota, was then arrested. The Georgia court, however, ordered his release on the grounds that, as an employee of the national government, he was exempt from the 1830 law. The governor persuaded Jackson to remove Worcester as postmaster. Georgia then ordered the missionary to leave the state. When he refused, he was arrested and sentenced to four years at hard labor. When he appealed the Georgia court decision to the Supreme Court, the state passed resolutions refusing to appear and denying the Court's authority. Wirt joined Worcester in bringing the case to the Supreme Court.

On March 3, 1832, Marshall ruled that all of Georgia's Indian laws were repugnant to the Constitution, laws, and treaties of the United States. The exclusive jurisdiction of the national government, he said, left no room for any state legislation affecting the Indians. That also included Worcester, who had been living on land guaranteed by treaty. Duval (who had been absent in 1831), Story, and Thompson joined the chief justice. McLean wrote a concurring opinion upholding Worcester's release but disagreeing with Marshall's vindication of Indian rights. Baldwin dissented, and Johnson was absent. Two days later the Court ordered Georgia to release Worcester.

"Thanks be to God," Story wrote his wife, "the Court can wash their hands clean of the iniquity of oppressing the Indians and disregarding their rights." The Court, the Cherokees, and Worcester were morally vindicated but still vulnerable. Actually, the Cherokees were no better off than in 1831 when Marshall had stated that it was up to the political branches of government to "redress wrongs or prevent the future." Even Worcester's fate depended upon Georgia's compliance with the Court's order or, in the event of a refusal, upon Jackson's enforcement.

To no one's surprise Georgia resisted. Worcester remained in jail. Jackson did nothing, but he was neither requested nor required to do anything. The Court's order required only Georgia's compliance. By the time news of Georgia's refusal reached Washington, the Court was no longer in session. No action was possible until January 1833.

By the fall of 1832 Marshall was despondent. July had produced not only Jackson's bank veto but also a new tariff which provoked talk of open rebellion in South Carolina. Georgia was still openly defiant. These ominous events and the passionate presidential contest caused the chief justice "to yield slowly and reluctantly to the conviction that our constitution cannot last." The Union, he wrote Story, "has been preserved thus far by miracles. I fear they cannot continue."

A minor miracle followed Jackson's handsome victory. In late November South Carolina passed a Nullification Ordinance invalidating the tariffs of 1828 and 1832, prohibiting any appeal to the Supreme Court, and threatening secession if the national government intervened. Jackson, however, would not tolerate defiance of a national law and said so unequivocally in a proclamation on December 10. Then, in his message to Congress, he requested a force bill giving federal courts and officials the power to deal with this emergency.

The great coming together to save the Union squeezed the Indians into the background—permanently, as it turned out. The Force Act remedied deficiencies that had prevented the Court from enforcing its decree against Georgia. Jackson's determined stand and a compromise tariff in 1833 induced South Carolina to suspend its Nullification Ordinance. Georgia pardoned Worcester. Story reported to his wife that since Jackson's proclamation and message to Congress "the Chief Justice and myself have become his warmest supporters. . . . Who would have dreamed of such an occurrence?"

Story was overly effusive. Marshall never warmly supported Jackson and remained alarmed at the antics of the Jacksonians. The nation had fallen on evil times, and South Carolina had only deferred secession until the other southern states were ready to join her.

Since the early 1820s the chief justice had compromised to preserve the Union and the Court. A final concession came during the 1833 term in *Barron* v. *Baltimore*, his last constitutional opinion.

A Baltimore program to construct and repair city streets diverted certain streams from their natural courses. The wayward streams began depositing sand and debris near the wharf owned by John Barron, making the water too shallow for ships to approach. Barron sued for damages and ultimately appealed to the Supreme Court on the grounds that the city's action violated the Fifth Amendment provision that private property could not be taken for public use without "just compensation." Baltimore admitted the damage to the wharf but denied liability, asserting that it had acted under authority of a state law. The single question before the Court was whether the Bill of Rights (the first eight amendments) limited state power. Marshall proceeded as if no controversy existed. The question, he said, was "of great importance, but not of much difficulty." The Bill of Rights limited only the national government. The Court had no jurisdiction. No justices dissented.

Barron was a poignant cap to the career of John Marshall, whose great decisions had expanded national power. But it was completely in character. Reconciled to the failure of his efforts to create a stable Union and a unified Court, he now sought only to hold both together. Illness and division so plagued the Court that at the close of the 1834 term Marshall postponed three cases then pending. He announced that the "practice of this Court is not (except in cases of absolute necessity) to deliver judgment in cases where constitutional questions are involved unless four judges concur in the opinion." The cases were continued again in 1835. To muster a majority on sensitive issues was impossible. Marshall was fast becoming a monument to a vanished age.

"Could I find the mill which would grind old men, and restore youth," he wrote in April 1835, "I might indulge the hope of recovering my former vigor and taste for the enjoyment of life. But as that is impossible, I must be content with patching myself up and dragging on as well as I can." Marshall was "dragging on" better than most. Though his pace slackened, he persisted in performing his judicial duties, published a two-volume edition of his *Life of George Washington,* and remained an active member of the Quoit Club at Richmond.

The vitality of his mind persisted, but his physical strength manifestly declined.

At the close of the 1835 term the seventy-nine-year-old chief justice injured his spine in a stagecoach accident on the return to Richmond. He also suffered from a diseased liver. Chancellor Kent visited him at Richmond in May and found him "very emaciated, feeble & dangerously low." In early June, aware that death was imminent, Marshall went to Philadelphia and consulted with Dr. Physick, who confirmed his suspicions. The chief justice spent his last days calmly and, in the fashion of the time, composed his epitaph. Then, on July 6, 1835, he died.

The entire nation mourned his passing as his body was taken to Richmond and buried beside Polly. Friend and foe alike eulogized his integrity, learning, and patriotism. Story, his close friend and associate for almost a quarter century, had written a more fitting epitaph in an 1833 letter dedicating his *Commentaries on the Constitution* to the chief justice. Marshall's "expositions of constitutional law" were "a monument of fame far beyond the memorials of political and military glory." They were the "victories of a mind accustomed to grapple with difficulties, capable of unfolding the most comprehensive truths with masculine simplicity and severe logic, and prompt to dissipate the illusions of ingenious doubt, and subtle argument, and impassioned eloquence."

The measure of Marshall's accomplishments was apparent when the Court opened its 1836 term. At his death the Constitution stood firmly as the supreme law of the Union, the Court had become a vital and respected organ of the government, and public anxiety and partisan maneuvering over the appointment of Marshall's successor was widespread. "His life," as Story said, spoke "its own best eulogy."

A Note on the Sources

JOHN MARSHALL was a careless record keeper who simply did not believe the records of his life worth preserving. The body of primary materials for Marshall's life will therefore never be large. Without the public records of his career as a lawyer, legislator, and chief justice, we would have only fragments, many gleaned from the more carefully preserved records of his correspondents. For over a decade the Institute of Early American History and Culture at Williamsburg has been gathering all extant Marshall materials for publication in a projected ten-volume series under the editorship of Herbert A. Johnson et al. The first three volumes of *The Papers of John Marshall* (Chapel Hill, N.C., 1974–1979) cover his life through his election to Congress in 1798 and are important both for the skillfully edited primary materials and the valuable editorial notes on such topics as his law practice, the Fairfax purchase, and the XYZ affair.

Until completion of the Marshall Papers project, primary sources about Marshall will remain scattered. Irwin S. Rhodes's *The Papers of John Marshall: A Descriptive Calendar* (2 vols., Norman, Okla., 1969) provides a comprehensive list of manuscript and printed sources for Marshall's life. For his brief sojourn in the Sixth Congress the *Annals of Congress* are the important source. His judicial opinions will be found in the official reports of cases argued and decided before the Supreme Court of the United States. Now published as *United States Reports,* these reports before 1875 issued under the reporters' names—for Marshall's career, 1 Cranch through 9 Peters. *The Federal Cases* contain his work on the circuit court. David Robertson's *Reports of the Trials of Colonel Aaron Burr* (2 vols., Philadelphia, 1808) is a stenographic account of that episode. In 1827 Marshall answered a request by Story and wrote a brief autobiography covering his life to his appointment to the Supreme Court. John Stokes Adams edited this work as *An Autobiographical Sketch by John Marshall* (Ann Arbor, 1937). A valuable primary source for Marshall's opinions on the events of his time is his *The Life of George Washington* (2 vol. ed., Philadelphia, 1836). Letters between Marshall and Story appear in two places: Charles C. Smith, ed., "Letters of Chief Justice Marshall," *Proceedings of the Massachusetts Historical Society,* 14 (1900), 320–360; and Charles Warren, "The Story–Marshall Correspondence (1819–1831)," *William and Mary Quarterly,* 21 (1941), 1–26. Some of Marshall's letters to Polly are in "Letters from John Marshall to His Wife," *William and Mary Quarterly,* 3 (1923), 73–90. Some of his newspaper essays and elucidating analyses are in Gerald Gunther, ed., *John Marshall's Defense of McCulloch v. Maryland* (Stanford, 1969). Some useful bits and pieces are found in John Edward Oster's impossibly organized and inaccurately edited *The Political and Economic Doctrines of John Marshall* (New York, 1914).

The papers of Marshall contemporaries fill some gaps. Two are particularly useful: Paul Leicester Ford, ed., *The Writings of Thomas Jefferson* (10 vols., New York, 1892–1899); and William Wetmore Story, ed., *Life and Letters of Joseph Story* (2 vols., Boston, 1851). Others are occasionally useful: Seth Ames, ed., *Works of Fisher Ames* (2 vols., Boston, 1854); John P. Kennedy, *Memoirs of the Life of William Wirt* (2 vols., New York, 1872); and Charles R. King, ed., *Life and Correspondence of Rufus King* (6 vols., New York, 1894–1900).

Some Marshall biographers were unconcerned with the dearth of information about his life, because they preferred to make him a symbol of the Court and praise or condemn accordingly. Veneration of the symbol dominated the nineteenth century and climaxed in 1901 when the bench and bar indulged in an orgy of adulation celebrating the centennial of Marshall's appointment as chief justice. John Forrest Dillon collected and edited these addresses in *John Marshall: Life, Character and Judicial Services* (3 vols., Chicago, 1903). The few dissenters were more concerned with attacking the use of judicial review to invalidate reform legislation in the late nineteenth and early twentieth centuries. Lacking primary evidence for Marshall, these critics began examining his times. James Bradley Thayer's *John Marshall* (Boston, 1901) was the first scholarly effort to promote John Marshall to mortality. The twentieth century heralded a critical reevaluation of Marshall. He remained the great chief justice, but scholars began asking whether talent or partisanship lay behind his greatness and whether he had impartially administered the law or used it for economic ends.

Albert J. Beveridge's monumental four-volume *The Life of John Marshall* (Boston, 1916–1919) was the first full-scale biography of Marshall in his times. Combining magnificent storytelling and prodigious research, the Progressive senator from Indiana turned Marshall's life into an epic of early America and added luster to the hero image. He also gave his epic hero a villain of equal dimension: Thomas Jefferson. It is history in the grand tradition with great men, archetypes, moving against a panoramic backdrop of problems and personalities and personifying divergent visions of America's future. Though one-sided, Beveridge remains unsurpassed. Edward S. Corwin's *John Marshall and the Constitution: A Chronicle of the Supreme Court* (New Haven, 1919) is a short, judicial biography in the Beveridge tradition.

World War I kindled interest in Jefferson, and praise for the apostle of human liberty joined criticism of the Court to start a movement debunking Marshall. Vernon L. Parrington's *Main Currents in American Thought* (2 vols., New York, 1927) is typical. Parrington called Marshall the "supreme materialist" who turned the "plastic" Constitution into an engine of capitalist exploitation. By the 1930s, however, a more balanced consensus percolated through the Marshall literature. Max Lerner, in a penetrating but admiring analysis, "John Marshall and the Campaign of History," *Columbia Law Review*, 20 (1939), 396–431, argued that Marshall used nationalism to link the eighteenth-century notion of the rule of law and the nineteenth century's rising industrialism—stressing the symbiosis of law and economic development. David Loth gives a lively anecdotal account in *Chief Justice Marshall and the Growth of the Republic* (New York, 1949) but is weak in analysis of cases. In the most recent full-scale biography, *John Marshall: A Life in Law* (New York, 1974), Leonard Baker provides a mine of information and captures the private and public drama in Marshall's life. Herbert A. Johnson's "John Marshall," in Leon Friedman and Fred Israel, eds., *The Justices of the Supreme Court, 1789–1969* (4 vols., New York, 1969), is an excellent short biography. See also the useful assessment of Marshall's work in the first chapter of G. Edward White's *The American Judicial Tradition: Profiles of Leading American Judges* (New York, 1976).

With the reexamination of Marshall came an investigation of the Supreme Court. Charles Beard's classic *The Supreme Court and the Constitution* (rev. ed., Englewood Cliffs, N.J., 1962) argues that Marshall only followed the intent of the Constitution's framers in using judicial review. Charles Warren's *The Supreme Court in United States History* (2 vols., Boston, 1922) credits Marshall with "vitalizing" the Constitution but concludes that he was out of touch with the times at his death. Warren is valuable, not for analysis of cases, but for the wide discussion of popular reaction to the Court's work and his recognition that the Court as an institution was influenced by the other justices and the bar. Louis Boudin's *Government by Judiciary* (2 vols., New York, 1932) is a massively documented effort to prove the Court a usurper. Although openly Jeffersonian, Charles G. Gaines is more balanced in *The Role of the Supreme Court in American Government and Politics* (Berkeley, 1944). He scolds Marshall for partisan behavior but praises him as a prime force in establishing Union. Three articles probe the inner working of the Marshall Court and shatter the notion that Marshall dominated the Court: Donald G. Morgan, "The Origin of Supreme Court Dissent," *William and Mary Quarterly,* 10 (1953), 353–377; Donald M. Roper, "Judicial Unanimity and the Marshall Court—A Road to Reappraisal," *American Journal of Legal History,* 9 (1965), 118–134; and Gerald Garvey, "The Constitutional Revolution of 1837 and the Myth of Marshall's Monolith," *Western Political Quarterly,* 18 (1965), 27–34. Robert G. McCloskey's *The American Supreme Court* (Chicago, 1960) offers a provocative discussion of the great cases of the Marshall years. R. Kent Newmyer's *The Supreme Court under Marshall and Taney* is a succinct, thorough, and penetrating examination of the Marshall Court in an historical context.

Special studies of Marshall and his Court abound. A complete list to the 1955 Marshall bicentennial is James A. Servies's *A Bibliography of John Marshall* (Washington, 1956). W. Melville Jones, ed., *Chief Justice John Marshall: A Reappraisal* (Ithaca, 1956) is a collection of articles by leading Marshall scholars seeking basically to discover whether anything new remained to be said about Marshall after two centuries. On Marshall's legal training see: Charles T. Cullen, "New Light on John Marshall's Legal Education and Admission to the Bar," *American Journal of Legal History,* 16 (1972), 345–351; and William F. Swindler, "John Marshall's Preparation for the Bar—Some

Observations on His Law Notes," *American Journal of Legal History,* 11 (1967), 207–213. The circumstances of Marshall's appointment as chief justice are covered thoroughly in Kathryn Turner's articles: "The Appointment of Chief Justice Marshall," *William and Mary Quarterly,* 18 (1960), 143–163; and "Federalist Policy and the Judiciary Act of 1801," *William and Mary Quarterly,* 22 (1965), 3–32. Richard Hooker corrects an often misquoted Marshall letter in "John Marshall on the Judiciary, the Republicans, and Jefferson, March 3, 1801," *American Historical Review,* 53 (1948), 518–520.

Controversy still swirls about judicial review and the decision in *Marbury.* The earliest investigations were: James Bradley Thayer, "The Origin and Scope of the American Doctrine of Constitutional Law," *Harvard Law Review,* 7 (1893), 129–156; and Edward S. Corwin, *The Doctrine of Judicial Review* (Princeton, 1914). Recently, Donald O. Dewey's *Marshall Versus Jefferson: The Political Background of Marbury v. Madison* (New York, 1970) explains the case as a victory for Marshall's cunning partisanship. In a more revisionist work, *The Jeffersonian Crisis: Courts and Politics in the Young Republic* (New York, 1971), Richard E. Ellis convincingly shows Jefferson and Marshall as moderates standing for an independent judiciary and against extremists in their respective parties. The old Marshall-versus-Jefferson theme also influenced accounts of the Burr trial until Robert K. Faulkner's "John Marshall and the Burr Trial," *Journal of American History,* 53 (1966), 247–258, put it to rest.

Felix Frankfurter brilliantly places the commerce clause in historical perspective in *The Commerce Clause under Marshall, Taney and Waite* (Chapel Hill, N.C., 1937). Benjamin Fletcher Wright's *The Contract Clause of the Constitution* (Cambridge, Mass., 1938) is the principal study of that Marshallian shield for property against state infringement. Cases are the raw material of constitutional law, and a number of case studies are pertinent to this study: C. Peter Magrath's *Yazoo, Law and Politics in the New Republic: The Case of Fletcher v. Peck* (Providence, 1966); Maurice G. Baxter, *The Steamboat Monopoly: Gibbons v. Ogden, 1824* (New York, 1970); Francis N. Stites, *Private Interest and Public Gain: The Dartmouth College Case, 1819* (Amherst, 1972); Joseph C. Burke, "The Cherokee Cases: A Study in Law, Politics, and Morality," *Stanford Law Review,* 21 (1969), 500–531; and John T. Noonan, Jr., *The Antelope* (Berkeley, 1977). Donald M. Roper questions what options were available to the justices in "In Quest of

Judicial Objectivity: The Marshall Court and the Legitimation of Slavery," *Stanford Law Review*, 21 (1969), 532–539. Maurice G. Baxter's *Daniel Webster and the Supreme Court* (Amherst, 1966) examines Webster's career to illustrate the important influence of the bar on the Supreme Court.

For a long time the glaring gap in twentieth-century Marshall scholarship was the failure to investigate and analyze his political principles. Morton Frisch deplored this failure in "John Marshall's Philosophy of Constitutional Republicanism," *The Review of Politics*, 20 (1958), 34–45. William Winslow Crosskey, in "John Marshall," in Allison Dunham and Philip B. Kurland, eds., *Mr. Justice* (Chicago, 1964), argues that Marshall was a strict constructionist struggling heroically to preserve the unitary state designed by the Founding Fathers in 1787. Julian P. Boyd, editor of the Jefferson Papers, argues similarly in "The Chasm That Separated Thomas Jefferson and John Marshall," in Gottfried Dietze, ed., *Essays on the American Constitution* (Englewood Cliffs, N.J., 1964). Boyd stresses Marshall's allegiance to Hamilton's philosophy of government. The connection between Marshall and Hamilton's ideas is better examined by Samuel J. Konefsky in *John Marshall and Alexander Hamilton: Architects of the American Constitution* (New York, 1964). Robert K. Faulkner's definitive *The Jurisprudence of John Marshall* (Princeton, 1968) shows that Marshall's principles were a hybrid of Lockean liberalism, Americanism, and Ciceronian respect for the decent gentleman and that the chief justice, unlike Hamilton, was not the prototypical modern leader.

Glimpses of the private Marshall are available in: Frances Norton Mason's *My Dearest Polly* (Richmond, 1961); Sallie E. Marshall Hardy's "John Marshall, Third Chief Justice of the United States, as Son, Brother, Husband, Friend," in *The Green Bag*, 8 (1896), 479–492; and Andrew Oliver's *The Portraits of John Marshall* (Charlottesville, Va., 1977).

Biographies of Marshall's contemporaries are essential to understanding the man in his times. Dumas Malone's *Jefferson and His Time* (5 vols., Boston, 1948–1974) is indispensable on Marshall's great adversary. On the Burr trial, though, see Garry Wills's corrective essay review "The Strange Case of Jefferson's Subpoena," *The New York Review of Books* (May 2, 1974), 15–19. Donald G. Morgan's *Justice William Johnson, the First Dissenter* (Columbia, S.C., 1954) is a fine biography of Jefferson's first appointee. Gerald T. Dunne's *Justice Joseph Story and the Rise of the Supreme Court* (New York, 1970) is the only biography of Marshall's close friend and colleague. Morton Borden's *The Federalism of James A. Bayard* (New York, 1955) helps illuminate issues during the Sixth Congress and the judiciary debates in 1801–1802. Also useful are: James T. Flexner, *Washington: The Indispensable Man* (4 vols., Boston, 1965–1970); Stephen G. Kurtz, *The Presidency of John Adams: The Collapse of Federalism* (New York, 1957); Harry Ammon, *James Monroe: The Quest for National Identity* (New York, 1971); Ralph Ketcham, *James Madison: A Biography* (New York, 1971); and Gertrude Wood, *William Paterson of New Jersey* (Fairlawn, N.J., 1933).

Charles S. Sydnor's *Gentlemen Freeholders: Political Practices in Washington's Virginia* (Chapel Hill, N.C., 1952) is the best introduction to the world of Marshall's youth. Marshall's place in the partisan struggles and party development of the 1790s is discussed in: Lisle A. Rose, *Prologue to Democracy: The Federalists in the South, 1789–1800* (Lexington, 1968); Richard R. Beeman, *The Old Dominion and the New Nation, 1788–1801* (Lexington, 1972); and Carl E. Prince, *The Federalists and the Origins of the U. S. Civil Service* (New York, 1977). Alexander DeConde's *The Quasi-War: The Politics and Diplomacy of the Undeclared War with France, 1797–1801* (New York, 1966) offers a good discussion of Marshall's mission to France. James Morton Smith's pro-Jeffersonian discussion of the Sedition Act, *Freedom's Fetters: The Alien and Sedition Laws and American Civil Liberties* (Ithaca, 1956) is offset in Leonard Levy's *Jefferson and Civil Liberties: The Darker Side* (Cambridge, Mass., 1963), which is also pertinent for the Burr trial. Thomas P. Abernethy's *The Burr Conspiracy* (New York, 1954) provides the best account of that episode. A lively account of the trial is found in Richard B. Morris's *Fair Trial* (New York, 1967). Bradley Chapin examines the most important result of that trial in *The American Law of Treason: Revolutionary and Early National Origins* (Seattle, 1964). Portions of Raoul Berger's three works are valuable on topics from Marshall's years: *Congress v. The Supreme Court* (Cambridge, Mass., 1969); *Impeachment: The Constitutional Problems* (Cambridge, Mass., 1973); and *Executive Privilege: A Constitutional Myth* (Cambridge, Mass., 1974).

Index